# my **revision** notes

## AS Edexcel History
# THE TRIUMPH OF FASCISM IN ITALY
## 1896–1943

Robin Bunce
Laura Gallagher
Sarah Ward

Orders: please contact Bookpoint Ltd, 130 Milton Park, Abingdon, Oxon OX14 4SB. Telephone: +44 (0)1235 827720. Fax: +44 (0)1235 400454. Lines are open 9.00a.m.–5.00p.m., Monday to Saturday, with a 24-hour message answering service. Visit our website at www.hoddereducation.co.uk.

© Robin Bunce, Laura Gallagher, Sarah Ward 2014
First published in 2014 by
Hodder Education,
An Hachette UK company
338 Euston Road
London NW1 3BH

Impression number    10  9  8  7  6  5  4  3  2
Year                 2018  2017  2016  2015  2014

Cover photo © Comugnero Silvana – Fotolia

Typeset in 11/13 Stempel Schneidler Std–Light by Datapage (India) Pvt. Ltd.
Artwork by Datapage (India) Pvt. Ltd
Printed and bound in India

A catalogue record for this title is available from the British Library

ISBN 978 1444 199567

# Contents

# Introduction

## About Unit 1

Unit 1 is worth 50 per cent of your AS level. It requires detailed knowledge of a historical period and the ability to explain the causes, consequences and significance of historical events. There are no sources in the Unit 1 exam and therefore all marks available are awarded for use of your own knowledge.

In the exam, you are required to answer two questions from a range of options. The questions are all worth 30 marks and therefore you should divide your time – including any extra time you have been allocated – equally between the questions.

The questions you answer must be on different topics. This book deals exclusively with topic E3: The Collapse of the Liberal State and the Triumph of Fascism in Italy, 1896–1943. However, you must also be prepared to answer a question on another topic.

The exam will test your ability to:

■ select information that focuses on the question

■ organise this information to provide an answer to the question

■ show range and depth in the examples you provide

■ analyse the significance of the information used to reach an overall judgement.

### The Collapse of the Liberal State and the Triumph of Fascism in Italy, 1896–1943

The exam board specifies that students should study four general areas as part of this topic.

1. Weaknesses of the political system and attempts to stabilise it from 1903 under Giolitti; social discontent and political disorder, 1896–1912.

2. The impact of the First World War on Italy and its impact on the Liberal State, 1918–23: Mussolini and the message and appeal of Fascism, 1919–22.

3. Power and control in Fascist Italy: propaganda; terror; the PNF (Partito Nazionale Fascista) economic policies; the relationship of the regime with the Church and the old elites.

4. Building the new Roman Empire, 1922–43: Abyssinia, Spain and Italy's diplomatic and military preparations for war, 1933–41.

## How to use this book

This book has been designed to help you to develop the knowledge and skills necessary to succeed in the exam. The book is divided into four sections – one for each general area of the course. Each section is made up of a series of topics organised into double-page spreads. On the left-hand page, you will find a summary of the key content you need to learn. Words in bold in the key content are defined in the glossary.

On the right-hand page, you will find exam-focused activities. Together, these two strands of the book will take you through the knowledge and skills essential for exam success.

▼ Key historical content                    ▼ Exam-focused activities

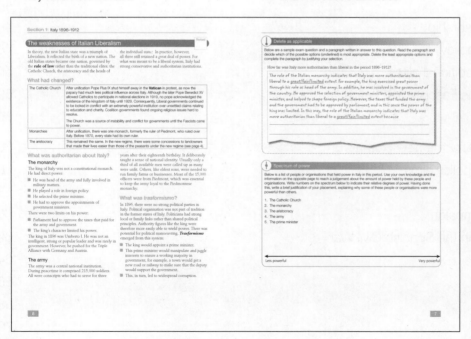

There are three levels of exam-focused activities.

- Band 1 activities are designed to develop the foundational skills needed to pass the exam. These have a turquoise heading and this symbol:

- Band 2 activities are designed to build on the skills developed in Band 1 activities and to help you to develop the skills necessary for a C grade. These have an orange heading and this symbol:

- Band 3 activities are designed to enable you to access the highest grades. These have a purple heading and this symbol:

Some of the activities have answers or suggested answers on pages 75–77 and have this symbol:

On pages 16–17, 34–35, 54–55 and 68–69 are four exam-style questions and model A-grade answer with examiner's commentary. This will give you guidance on what is expected to achieve the top grade.

You can also keep track of your revision by ticking off each topic heading in the book, or by ticking the checklist on the contents page. Tick each box when you have:

- revised and understood a topic
- completed the activities.

# Mark scheme

For some of the activities in the book it will be useful to refer to the mark scheme for the unit. Below is the mark scheme for Unit 1.

| Level | Marks | Description |
|-------|-------|-------------|
| 1 | 1–6 | • Lacks focus on the question<br>• Limited factual accuracy<br>• Highly generalised<br>*Level 1 answers are highly simplistic, irrelevant or vague.* |
| 2 | 7–12 | • General points with some focus on the question<br>• Some accurate and relevant supporting evidence<br>*Level 2 answers might tell the story without addressing the question, or address the question without providing supporting examples.* |
| 3 | 13–18 | • General points that focus on the question<br>• Accurate support, but this may be either only partly relevant or lacking detail, or both<br>• Attempted analysis<br>*Level 3 answers attempt to focus on the question, but have significant areas of weakness. For example, the focus on the question may drift, the answer may lack specific examples, or parts of the essay may simply tell the story. Answers that do not deal with factors that are stated in the question cannot achieve higher than Level 3.* |
| 4 | 19–24 | • General points that clearly focus on the question and show understanding of the most important factors involved<br>• Accurate, relevant and detailed supporting evidence<br>• Analysis<br>*Level 4 answers clearly attempt to answer the question and demonstrate a detailed and wide-ranging knowledge of the period studied.* |
| 5 | 25–30 | • As Level 4<br>• Sustained analysis<br>*Level 5 answers are thorough and detailed. They clearly engage with the question and offer a balanced and carefully reasoned argument, which is sustained throughout the essay.* |

# Section 1:
## Italy 1896–1912

### A new country

Italy was a very new country in 1896. Although it had a long and rich history, it suffered from many problems as a result of its late development. **Unification** (which took place in 1870) had happened quickly and had brought together two very different areas:

- the wealthy and more industrially developed North and
- the poor and agricultural South.

The South did not feel like it was a part of the new Italy as all of the political power and wealth was in the North. Italy also suffered by comparison to the other powers of Europe, as it did not possess an empire and remained unrecognised by the Pope, who had lost lands and power because of the **Risorgimento**.

### Social and economic conditions in Italy in 1896

| Condition | Socio-economic result |
|---|---|
| Compared to other countries (especially the second newest country, Germany), Italy was poor and economically underdeveloped. | Agricultural labourers earned under 50p per week; income per head was under £8 per year in Italy compared to £26 in France and £31 in Britain. |
| Agriculture was by far the biggest employer but there were wide variations in the patterns of agriculture. | Nearly 60 per cent of the population worked on the land – in Britain only 10 per cent did. Farms varied from small-scale peasant agriculture in the Alps to vast estates in the south owned by aristocratic landowners. |
| The revolution had challenged the old class structure but this just meant that the aristocracy now shared power with the new middle class elite. | The intention to build new networks of independent (and wealthier) peasant farmers was not realised; when **feudal laws** were abolished, lawyers and local government officials benefited. |

### What was life like for the poor?

- Disease was rife – malaria was particularly widespread in the south of Italy, killing 15,000 people annually. The water supply was often infected and many died of cholera.
- Poor diet – in the North the diet of the poor was based on polenta. The lack of variety led to vitamin deficiencies and the disease **pellagra**. Few of Italy's poor could afford luxury foods like tomatoes, cheese and ham. Most wine was sold to the middle class or went for export.
- Housing conditions were primitive – often one- or two-bedroom houses for large families, which they shared with their animals.

### Who were the middle and upper classes of the new Italy?

- The old elite were the noble aristocratic families. There were 7387 noble families, many more than in Britain. Sicily alone had 208 princes.
- Nobility did not automatically entail wealth. Some did still own large estates and were more enterprising, but many others relied on income from jobs like army officers that were not particularly well paid.
- After unification, there were approximately 200,000 landowners and businessmen with whom the nobility had to share power. Lawyers and doctors were also landowners and they dominated local government. These people formed the basis of the new middle class.
- There were around 250,000 non-manual government workers, of which 75,000 were teachers. They were not very highly paid. The jobs were secure, however, which caused them to value the work more than they might have otherwise.

## Spider diagram

Use the information on the opposite page to add detail to the spider diagram below.

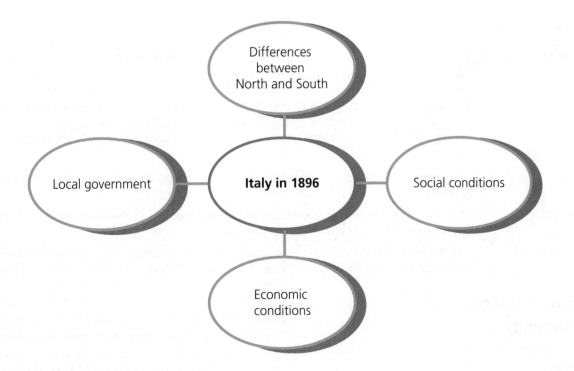

## Complete the table

The Liberal regime in Italy collapsed in 1922. Many historians believe that the reasons for its collapse can be dated back to the end of the nineteenth century. Use the information on the opposite page to complete the table below. In the left-hand column, list factors that made Italy difficult to govern in 1896. In the right-hand column explain how each factor made Italy difficult to govern.

| Factor | How did this make Italy difficult to govern? |
|--------|-----------------------------------------------|
|        |                                               |
|        |                                               |
|        |                                               |
|        |                                               |

## The weaknesses of Italian Liberalism

In theory, the new Italian state was a triumph of Liberalism. It reflected the birth of a new nation. The old Italian states became one nation, governed by the **rule of law** rather than the traditional elites: the Catholic Church, the aristocracy and the heads of the individual states. In practice, however, all three still retained a great deal of power. For what was meant to be a liberal system, Italy had strong conservative and authoritarian institutions.

### What had changed?

| | |
|---|---|
| The Catholic Church | After unification Pope Pius IX shut himself away in the **Vatican** in protest, as now the papacy had much less political influence across Italy. Although the later Pope Benedict XV allowed Catholics to participate in national elections in 1919, no pope acknowledged the existence of the kingdom of Italy until 1929. Consequently, Liberal governments continued to be locked in conflict with an extremely powerful institution over unsettled claims relating to education and charity. Coalition governments found ongoing religious issues hard to resolve. |
| | The Church was a source of instability and conflict for governments until the Fascists came to power. |
| Monarchies | After unification, there was one monarch, formerly the ruler of Piedmont, who ruled over Italy. Before 1870, every state had its own ruler. |
| The aristocracy | This remained the same. In the new regime, there were some concessions to landowners that made their lives easier than those of the peasants under the new regime (see page 4). |

### What was authoritarian about Italy?

#### The monarchy

The king of Italy was not a constitutional monarch. He had direct power:

- He was head of the army and fully involved in military matters.
- He played a role in foreign policy.
- He selected the prime minister.
- He had to approve the appointments of government ministers.

There were two limits on his power:

- Parliament had to approve the taxes that paid for the army and government.
- The king's character limited his power.

The king in 1896 was Umberto I. He was not an intelligent, strong or popular leader and was rarely in government. However, he pushed for the Triple Alliance with Germany and Austria.

#### The army

The army was a central national institution. During peacetime it comprised 215,000 soldiers. All were conscripts who had to serve for three years after their eighteenth birthday. It deliberately taught a sense of national identity. Usually only a third of all available men were called up as many were unfit. Others, like eldest sons, were needed to run family farms or businesses. Most of the 15,000 officers were from Piedmont, which was essential to keep the army loyal to the Piedmontese monarchy.

### What was *trasformismo*?

In 1896, there were no strong political parties in Italy. Political organisation was not part of tradition in the former states of Italy. Politicians had strong local or family links rather than shared political principles. Authority figures like the king were therefore more easily able to wield power. There was potential for political manoeuvring. **Trasformismo** emerged from this system:

- The king would appoint a prime minister.
- This prime minister would manipulate and juggle interests to ensure a working majority in government, for example, a town would get a new road or railway to make sure that the deputy would support the government.
- This, in turn, led to widespread corruption.

##  Delete as applicable

Below are a sample exam question and a paragraph written in answer to this question. Read the paragraph and decide which of the possible options (underlined) is most appropriate. Delete the least appropriate options and complete the paragraph by justifying your selection.

How far was Italy more authoritarian than liberal in the period 1896–1912?

> The role of the Italian monarchy indicates that Italy was more authoritarian than liberal to a <u>great/fair/limited</u> extent. For example, the king exercised great power through his role as head of the army. In addition, he was involved in the government of the country. He approved the selection of government ministers, appointed the prime minister, and helped to shape foreign policy. However, the taxes that funded the army and the government had to be approved by parliament, and in this sense the power of the king was limited. In this way, the role of the Italian monarchy indicates that Italy was more authoritarian than liberal to a <u>great/fair/limited</u> extent because
>
> _____
>
> _____

##  Spectrum of power

Below is a list of people or organisations that held power in Italy in this period. Use your own knowledge and the information on the opposite page to reach a judgement about the amount of power held by these people and organisations. Write numbers on the spectrum below to indicate their relative degrees of power. Having done this, write a brief justification of your placement, explaining why some of these people or organisations were more powerful than others.

1. The Catholic Church
2. The monarchy
3. The aristocracy
4. The army
5. The prime minister

Less powerful &harr; Very powerful

# Italy's economic boom 1896–1912

Between 1896 and 1912, Italy's economy surged. Italy's industrial revolution following 1896, during the '**Giolitti period**', resulted in a new political stability as the Italian people associated liberalism with economic success. In spite of the boom, however, there were underlying economic problems.

## Economic transformation

Under Prime Minister **Giovanni Giolitti** (see page 14), there was a period of considerable economic growth. Italian **Gross Domestic Product (GDP)** grew at an annual average of 2.8 per cent between 1896 and 1912. This growth was more impressive than both Britain and France at the time, where growth was less than 2 per cent a year.

## Causes of industrial growth

Several factors contributed to the economic boom prior to the First World War:

- A thriving European market which increased the demand for Italian goods.

- Emigration: between 1900 and 1910, six million Italians left Italy – but sent money to their relatives at home.

- Government spending on the military and hydro-electric dams boosted industrial production.

- Relatively low tariffs helped the trade of industrial goods and **raw materials**.

## Industrial growth

Economic growth was primarily driven by industrial growth, especially in the **new industries** between 1901 and 1914. For example, cheaper iron and steel imports led to the foundation of motor and engineering companies such as Fiat, Isotta Fraschinin Alfa, and Lancia between 1899 and 1906. Additionally, Pirelli and Montecatini began producing products such as sulphuric acid, rubber and electrical cables. The profits from new industries grew by 10.6 per cent between 1896 and 1913. By 1912 Italy was also producing more electricity than France, and had almost caught up with Britain's electrical production. Despite this, iron and steel production remained far below that of Britain and Germany.

More traditional industries such as textile production also boomed. For example, cotton production doubled between 1900 and 1908, and by 1912 Italy controlled 30 per cent of the global silk market.

## Problems in agriculture

There was some growth in agriculture too. On average, agriculture grew 2 per cent a year between 1896 and 1912. The sugar industry was particularly successful. Growth in sugar beet farming meant that sugar production grew from 6000 tons in 1898 to 130,000 tons in 1903.

More generally, however, agricultural production lagged behind industrial production. Wool production stagnated due to strikes among agricultural workers and a lack of modern machinery.

Many workers left agricultural production to work in industry or the **service sector**. Between 1897 and 1912 the proportion of workers who worked in agriculture dropped from 64 per cent to 58 per cent.

## Inequalities

From 1896 to 1912, Italian people grew richer by around 2.1 per cent a year on average. Industrial workers did particularly well. Their income rose by around 40 per cent between 1900 and 1912. This increase was considerably better than that of Britain, France, Austria, Germany and Japan. Rural incomes barely improved, however, accentuating inequalities between the country and the city. Moreover, Italians were still relatively poor: in 1912, the income of the average Italian household was only half that of the average French household.

## Economic and politics 1896–1912

Economic growth led to political stability. Giolitti enjoyed the support of major industrialists. Relatively high rates of wage growth also reduced the appeal of Marxist revolutionaries among the working class. The political stability and absence of opposition meant that Giolitti was not put under pressure to reform Italian politics. Giolitti's political reforms (see page 14) were, therefore, introduced very slowly and left many problems unsolved.

## Develop the detail

Below are a sample exam question and a paragraph written in answer to this question. The paragraph contains a limited amount of detail. Annotate the paragraph to add additional detail to the answer.

How far were economic problems the main cause of social discontent in Italy in the period 1896–1912?

> Economic problems played some role in creating social discontent in Italy in the period 1896–1912. Although industrial workers benefited from industrial growth, agricultural workers suffered in this period. For example, some industries suffered from a lack of modern machinery. In addition, many agricultural workers left to work in industry. Overall, incomes in rural areas of Italy barely increased. In this way, economic problems contributed to social discontent in Italy in the period 1896–1914 because they decreased standards of living for agricultural workers, and accentuated the divide between urban and rural areas.

## Introducing an argument

Below are a sample exam question, a list of key points to be made in the essay, and a simple introduction and conclusion for the essay. Read the question, the plan, the introduction and conclusion. Rewrite the introduction and the conclusion in order to develop an argument.

How far were economic problems the main cause of social discontent in Italy in the period 1896–1912?

**Key points**

- Economic problems
- Political problems
- Divisions between the North and the South
- Social divisions

**Introduction**

> There were four key causes of social discontent in Italy in the period 1896–1914. These were economic problems, political problems, divisions between the North and the South, and social divisions.

**Conclusion**

> There were four key causes of social discontent in Italy in the period 1896–1914. The most important reason was economic problems. This played a more significant role than all of the other factors.

## Regional divisions

National unity was undermined by the differences between the regions and the strong local identities. The north and south of Italy were very different. As discussed on page 4, the North was wealthier and more industrialised whereas the South was mostly agricultural and had much higher levels of poverty. The South felt alienated from the rest of Italy.

### Why did the South feel alienated?

- **Dialect** and language: The Italian language and the dialects spoken varied widely in different parts of the country. The Italian spoken in Sicily (in the South) is different from that spoken in Tuscany (in the North). Also, dialects were much more widely used in the nineteenth century. What is now called Italian was simply the dialect of Tuscany, the province that centred on Florence. In the 1890s only 2 per cent of the population spoke Italian. The language of Italian politics and power was that of the North, meaning that the people in the South found it hard to identify with the new state. These issues around language meant that it was hard for Italy to develop a unified sense of identity.

- Unification or conquest? Southerners felt that 'unification' was actually a conquest by Piedmont, the dominant northern state and the home province of the King of Italy. This left lasting resentment and bitterness in the South, and the general feeling that 'Italy' was just the product of another foreign invasion. In this sense southern resentment undermined the new Liberal regime because they did not feel part of the new state.

- Tax: The old rulers of southern Italy were inefficient tax-collectors. The taxes under the new state were higher and more efficiently collected. The livestock of the poor (mules, donkeys) were also more heavily taxed than the cattle of the rich, as the new Italian government felt that it had to appease the wealthy rather than the poor.

- Education and the vote: There was also an educational divide between the North and the South. This was very important because the **electoral franchise** was based on literacy after 1882. The introduction of compulsory schooling in the late 1880s had very little effect in the South, as there were truancy rates of around 80 per cent and therefore high illiteracy rates. Nonetheless, in more prosperous areas there was a considerable improvement. In Sicily, for example, the proportion of students at primary school shot up from 55 per cent in 1901 to 74 per cent in 1906.

- Corruption: The South still had 203 MPs out of 508 despite having a much smaller percentage of the electorate. Governments, therefore, relied heavily on the support of southern deputies, who could be more easily bribed or manipulated than their northern colleagues (who had larger electorates). This was part of the system of 'trasformismo' (see page 6).

### The impact of regionalism

Regionalism impacted on Liberal Italy by undermining the unity of the nation. Overall, between 1896 and 1912 regional identity was more important than national identity. For many, fear of losing their regional identify meant that Italians were unwilling to see themselves as fully Italian.

Below are a sample exam question and a paragraph written in answer to this question. Why does this paragraph not get into Level 4? Once you have identified the mistake, rewrite the paragraph so that it displays the qualities of Level 4. The mark scheme on page 3 will help you.

How far is it accurate to describe Italy as 'unified' in the period 1896–1912?

> One way in which Italy could not be described as 'unified' in the period 1896–1912 was in terms of education and voting rights. There were significant differences between literacy rates in the North and the South. This had an impact on voting rights as people who were illiterate could not register to vote. In this sense, Italy could not be described as 'unified' as people in the North were better educated and had greater political influence than those in the South.

Below are a sample exam question and a paragraph written in answer to this question. Read the paragraph and identify parts of the paragraph that are not directly relevant to the question. Draw a line through the information that is irrelevant and justify your deletions in the margin.

To what extent did regional differences in Italy undermine the unity of the Liberal State in the period 1896–1912?

> One way in which regional differences in Italy did undermine the unity of the Liberal State in the period 1896-1912 was through dialect and language. People in different parts of the country spoke different forms of Italian, with the Italian spoken in the North differing considerably from the Italian spoken in the South. The South was also much poorer as it was predominantly agricultural and grain prices had fallen. In the 1890s, only 2 per cent of the Italian population spoke Italian, while 98 per cent spoke in local dialects. Language differences had a twofold impact on the unity of the Liberal State. First, differences in language made it difficult for Italy to develop a sense of identity. Secondly, as political power was based in the North, the language of politics was that of the North. The King of Piedmont, Umberto I, had become King of Italy following unification even though he was unpopular and not very intelligent. Consequently, many in the South found it hard to identify with the government. In this way, regional differences in the form of language and dialect did undermine the unity of the Liberal State in the period 1896–1912 as they prevented many people from understanding or associating themselves with the new state.

## Italy as a world power and Italian nationalism

International relations in the late nineteenth century were dominated by European empires. Britain and France, the greatest nations in Europe, had the largest empires. Following unification Italy, like Germany and other younger nations, attempted to establish itself as a great power by creating an empire. Indeed, the creation of an Italian Empire was essential to the project of creating an Italian national identity.

However, Italy was never able to rival the British or French Empires and this had consequences for the aspirations of Italian nationalists.

### Francesco Crispi

Francesco Crispi, Prime Minister from 1887 to 1891 and again from 1893 to 1896, attempted to create a new national identity and to enhance Italy's status as a world power. He hoped that Italians would unite around a common mission to build an Italian Empire.

- In order to create a national identity he began to associate the Italian nation with popular heroes such as **Garibaldi** and **Mazzini**.
- He attempted to found an empire in Africa. His campaign, the First African War, which lasted from 1895 to 1896, was an attempt to win control of Abyssinia.

The First African War ended in disaster for Italy. Italy's army was defeated by a much larger Abyssinian force at Adowa on 1 March 1896. Around 7000 Italian troops were killed and some of the living prisoners were castrated. This represented a humiliation for Italy – the only European power to be defeated in this way while aiming to build an empire. Back in Italy there were protests all over the country demanding Crispi's resignation.

### Italy and the European empires

Compared to Britain, France and Germany, Italy was a weak nation. She was behind the other countries economically and had a smaller population. Indeed, by 1913 Britain was producing 16.2 million tons of iron and steel and Germany 28.6 million tons. Italy was far behind these two greatest industrial powers, producing only 0.6 million tons of iron and steel. Defeat in Abyssinia emphasised Italy's weakness.

### Nationalism and the Libyan War

In spite of the defeat in Abyssinia there was a growing Italian nationalist movement in the years before the First World War. The nationalists were strongly critical of the existing Italian government. They demanded:

- new attempts to create an Italian Empire
- tough anti-union policies.

From 1909 the movement grew, especially amongst the young and the well-educated. It became a destabilising force in Italy after 1909. The movement held a Nationalist Congress in 1910 and published the first issue of their journal, *L'idea Nazionale*, on 1 March 1911.

In 1911, Giolitti (see page 14) attempted to win the support of the nationalists by launching a campaign to capture Libya. The campaign was a disaster. The war was more difficult and expensive than planned, and Italy only succeeded in capturing Libya's coastal regions. Furthermore, the war failed to win the support of the nationalists who believed that Giolitti had done too little. At the same time, the war turned socialists and many Catholics against Giolitti as they objected to the violent imperialist policy.

### The impact of Italian nationalism on Italian government

Italian nationalism attracted many intellectuals, industrialists, journalists, and conservatives. Although nationalist groups were relatively small they were highly influential. Nationalism undermined Giolitti's Liberal government by advocating war in Libya, a policy that led to political **polarisation**.

## Spectrum of significance

Below are a sample exam question and a list of general points which could be used to answer the question. Use your own knowledge and the information on the opposite page to reach a judgement about the importance of these general points to the question posed. Write numbers on the spectrum below to indicate their relative importance. Having done this, write a brief justification of your placement, explaining why some of these factors are more important than others. The resulting diagram could form the basis of an essay plan.

How far was Italy's attempt to become a great power the main cause of social discontent in Italy in the period 1896–1912?

1. Italy's attempt to become a great power
2. Economic problems
3. The weaknesses of Italian liberalism
4. Divisions between North and South
5. Social divisions
6. The influence of the nationalist movement

Less important ←——————————————————————→ Very important

## Simple essay style

Below is a sample exam question. Use your own knowledge and the information on the opposite page to produce a plan for this question. Choose four general points, and provide three pieces of specific information to support each general point. Once you have planned your essay, write the introduction and conclusion for the essay. The introduction should list the points to be discussed in the essay. The conclusion should summarise the key points and justify which point was the most important.

How far does the influence of the nationalist movement in Italy account for the weaknesses of the Liberal State in the period 1896–1912?

## Giolitti's reforms

### Who was Giolitti?

Giovanni Giolitti was a Liberal politician. He was Prime Minister four times between 1903 and 1914 and once again in 1920–1921. Giolitti came to prominence after a period of instability in Italy caused by the repression of violent riots in May 1897, and the fall of the previous charismatic leader Crispi following the defeat at Adowa in 1896. He was a skilled political manipulator, adept at forming **coalitions** and using *trasformismo* (see page 6) to get parliament to pass his policies. He was criticised for his willingness to ally with anyone to achieve his aims. In 1921 he even offered Mussolini and the Fascists an electoral alliance. As Giolitti had been in power for such a long time, he had huge influence because he had appointed most of the key officials in government.

### What reforms did Giolitti make?

Giolitti's reforms aimed to broaden the appeal of the government, improve infrastructure and stimulate the economy.

- Between 1900 and 1907, spending on infrastructure and public works increased by 50 per cent. This included road-building, aqueducts, railway improvements and **irrigation schemes**.
- Child labour was banned and women's working hours were reduced to a maximum of 11 hours a day.
- National insurance provision for the sick and the elderly was extended. In 1907, Giolitti introduced a compulsory rest day and in 1910, a maternity fund. Families were paid 40 lire for every new baby.
- Strict neutrality was introduced for state agencies (such as the police) in the case of strikes.
- **Real wages** went up in agriculture and industry. This represented a genuine improvement in living standards for the poorest workers.

- The electoral franchise expanded from 3 million to 8.5 million. From 1912, all literate men over 21 had the right to vote, and all men over 30 could vote whether literate or not. It was much harder now to form the kind of coalitions and deals that had resulted from such a small electoral franchise and tight government control.

### Why did Giolitti fall in 1914?

- He faced radical opposition from the Left and the Right. Both sides wanted to change Italy, through violence if necessary. The Left called for a revolution to bring 'the people' to power. The Right wanted Italy cleansed by blood to rid it of 'corrupt elements'.
- Giolitti's labour reforms and the neutrality rule alienated the nationalists, who also criticised him for his foreign policy.
- The **Libyan War of 1911–12** was intended to unite the nation and stave off criticism, but it was expensive, brutal, and difficult to win and people blamed Giolitti for this. The nationalists received credit for the eventual victory. Giolitti resigned in March 1914, and was replaced by the more right-wing **Antonio Salandra**, who then took Italy into the First World War.

### The impact of Giolitti on Italian government

Giolitti's reforms changed the way that Italian government worked. Extending the electoral franchise undermined the Liberals' control on government because now the traditional *trasformismo* system was more difficult to sustain. It weakened the hold of the traditional elites as many more men now had the ability to determine their own vote. Living standards and real wages rose under Giolitti, and brought moderate socialists under the wing of the government, but this was not good enough to appease the nationalist movement.

## RAG – Rate the timeline

Below are a sample exam question and a timeline. Read the question, study the timeline and, using three coloured pens, put a red, amber or green star next to the events to show:

- red – events and policies that have no relevance to the question
- amber – events and policies that have some significance to the question
- green – events and policies that are directly relevant to the question

1) How far do you agree that Giolitti's government created political stability in the years 1903–14?

Now repeat the activity with the following questions. You could use different colours, or number your stars 1, 2 and 3.

2) How far were economic problems the main cause of social discontent in Italy in the period 1896–1914?

3) How far is it accurate to describe Italy as 'unified' in the period 1896–1914?

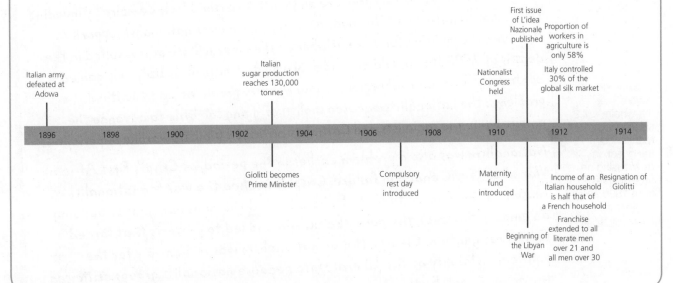

## Recommended reading

Below is a list of suggested further reading on this topic.

- *Italy: The Rise of Fascism 1915–1945*, chapter 2, Mark Robson (2006)
- *Modern Italy, 1871 to the Present*, pages 15–213, Martin Clark (2008)
- *A Concise History of Italy*, pages 143–188, Christopher Duggan (1994)

## Exam focus

Below is a sample A grade essay. Read it and the comments around it.

How far was the impact of Italian nationalism the main cause of the political instability of the Liberal State in the years 1896–1912?

This is a focused introduction that outlines the structure of the rest of the essay.

Italian nationalism was certainly one reason for the political instability of the Liberal State in the years 1896–1912. However, there were other problems that undermined the Liberal State, such as regional differences, the nature of Italy's economy, and Italy's political leadership.

Italian nationalism, particularly in the years following 1909, played a key role undermining the stability of the Liberal State. Nationalists undermined the state in several ways. First, they were critical of important aspects of government policy. For example, they wanted a renewed focus on building an Italian Empire in Africa, as well as tougher policies against Italy's unions. Second, they destabilised the government by putting pressure on Giolitti to extend Italy's empire by invading Libya. Giolitti authorised the invasion to try to win over nationalist support. However, the invasion further destabilised the Liberal State as it resulted in the deaths of 7,000 Italian soldiers and only a partial victory, as Italy only gained control of Libya's coastal regions. These military problems led to political problems: the nationalists accused Giolitti of doing too little to advance the empire while the socialists and Catholics criticised Giolitti's warlike imperialism.

The paragraph covers the whole time period mentioned in the question by focusing on an example from 1896 and another that followed 1909.

Nationalism was also a problem earlier in the period, as Crispi's First African War of 1895–96 ended in failure. Crispi launched the war for nationalist reasons, as he wanted to unite Italians behind the common goal of building an empire. However, the policy backfired and led to protests that forced Crispi's resignation. Clearly, Italian nationalism was responsible for the political instability of the Liberal State because nationalist groups criticised the government. Furthermore, nationalism inspired leaders to launch risky imperialist wars that ended in disaster for Italy.

Other factors also caused political instability in Liberal Italy. Regional divisions led to political problems. Although Crispi and other politicians tried to create a sense of national identity, regional identity was often more important than national identity. There were huge economic differences between the relatively industrially developed North, and the South that was still dominated by farming. Political unification did nothing to unite the poor rural workers of the South with the relatively wealthy industrial workers and rich middle class of the North. Additionally, Southerners tended to feel that unification was nothing more than a northern takeover which handed power to the Piedmont monarchy. Indeed, most of the Army's 15,000 officers were from Piedmont and Italian, the new national language, was rarely spoken in the South, again emphasising the feeling that national government were essentially foreign invaders. The strength of regional identity and the North–South divide clearly led to political instability of the Liberal State because a large section of society felt much more loyalty to their region than they did to the government of their nation.

The nature of Italy's economy also undermined the stability of the Liberal State. First, Italy's economy was poor compared to other major European powers. For example, in 1896, Italy was still a primarily agricultural country with nearly 60 per cent of its population working on farms. Britain by comparison was a primarily agricultural country with only 10 per cent of its population working on the land. Even with the massive economic growth of the Giolitti period, Italy was still producing only 0.6 million tons of iron and steel, compared to Germany's 28.6 million tons and Britain's 16.2 million tons. This meant that Italy did not have the resources to compete with Britain and Germany in terms of expanding its empire in Africa. In this sense, Italy's economic weaknesses contributed to the frustration of nationalists who wanted an Italian Empire. Economic growth also contributed to regionalism as industry in the North grew much more quickly than agriculture in the South. Rapid growth between 1900 and 1912 led to a 40 per cent rise in the income of industrial workers. However, agricultural growth was not as good due to the lack of modern machinery. Clearly, the nature of the economy led to a lack of stability in Italy's economy as it could not support successful imperial expansion and it made regional differences worse.

Finally, Italy's political leaders also played a part in undermining the stability of the Liberal State. Crispi's imperial policy undermined the stability of the state, due to Italy's failure in Abyssinia. The defeat at Adowa in 1896 led to the fall of his government in May 1897. Giolitti also made mistakes. Significantly, although the economic growth of 1896–1912 led to political stability, he did not use this period of calm to introduce major reforms. For example, he failed to resolve the relationship between Italy and the Roman Catholic Church. Additionally, he did not resolve the problems between North and South, and his electoral reforms that finally gave all men over the age of 30 the vote were only passed in 1912. Finally, in 1911, Giolitti unwisely launched the Libyan War which led to increased political polarisation rather than support for the Liberal State. Clearly, political leaders were also responsible for undermining the stability of the Liberal State because they made significant mistakes that made Italy's problems worse.

In conclusion, Italian nationalism did lead to the political instability of the Liberal State in the years 1896–1912. However, had economic circumstances been different and political leaders been wiser, nationalism might not have been such a big problem.

This paragraph shows how Italy's economy influenced the other factors mentioned in the essay. In so doing it achieved sustained analysis.

Again, this paragraph uses examples from throughout the period mentioned in the question showing a good range of knowledge.

The conclusion begins to show how economics affected other factors. Greater consideration of these links could have pushed the mark higher in Level 5.

27/30

This is a Level 5 essay due to the fact that it achieves sustained analysis through showing how the different factors relate. The focus on the question is strong throughout the essay and there is a good level of detail. A stronger introduction and conclusion that showed more explicitly how the different factors affected each other would have led to a higher mark.

## Reverse engineering

The best essays are based on careful plans. Read the essay and the examiner's comments and try to work out the general points of the plan used to write the essay. Once you have done this, note down the specific examples used to support each general point.

# Section 2:
# The impact of the First World War 1918–23

## Italy's 'mutilated victory'

Revised

### What was the 'mutilated victory'?

This term originated with the nationalist writer **Gabriele D'Annunzio** (see page 26). It reflects the popular Italian view that Italy deserved more from the Paris Peace Conference (1919) for its part in the war effort.

### What did Italy demand and what did it receive?

The Italian negotiators were in a difficult situation. They had to be realistic, yet were aware of the common desire, driven by D'Annunzio and other nationalists, to demand extensive territorial gains. The resulting **Treaty of St Germain** (1919) was almost bound to disappoint.

### How were the decisions made at St Germain?

The USA, Britain and France thought that Italy's demands in the Treaty of London were excessive. It didn't help that the Treaty of London was a secret agreement. Its signatories had not informed President Wilson about its contents. Thus the Treaty of St Germain was based on Wilson's '**Fourteen Points**' instead, three of which contradicted the Treaty of London. These were:

- Open diplomacy
- Italy's borders to be amended along nationalist lines
- Autonomy for the peoples of Austria–Hungary.

| Italian demands | The results of the Treaty of St Germain |
| --- | --- |
| **The Adriatic port of Fiume.** This was a nationalist demand. It did not feature in the **Treaty of London** that drew Italy into the Entente in May 1915. | This was not delivered. The US President Wilson believed this demand infringed **national self-determination.** Fiume had a mixed Italian and Croat population and so formed part of the new Yugoslavia, which the Entente wanted as a strong barrier against future German expansion. |
| The territories of South Tyrol, the Trentino, Istria and some of Dalmatia. These were all promised to Italy in the Treaty of London. | South Tyrol, Trentino and Istria were delivered but Dalmatia was not. The Dalmatian coast was ethnically Slav. It was given to the newly created Yugoslavia. |
| **Overseas colonies.** Nationalists believed Italy should share in the redistribution of Germany and Turkey's colonies | This was denied – it was thought this demand was far in excess of what Italy had contributed to the war effort. |

### What were Italian views on the Treaty of St Germain and how did this affect the Liberal government?

Many Italians were unhappy with the peace settlement:

- They believed that the Entente powers had denied Italy's demands for their own selfish motives.
- They also blamed the Italian government for abandoning the national interest.
- They believed that liberal democracy had failed them, particularly in terms of **expansionism**.
- **Demobilised** soldiers were particularly angry, seeing the peace settlement as an insufficient reward for their efforts in the war.
- The conservatives were also afraid and angry that the anti-war Socialist Party was threatening to take control.

### How justified were these views?

- Britain and France had sacrificed more in terms of people and resources during the First World War, and aided Italy in 1917 by sending extra troops to the Italian front. They thought Italy had not made a significant enough contribution to justify their demands.
- The Italian negotiator, Prime Minister Orlando, was no match for the British and French negotiators (David Lloyd George for Britain, Georges Clemenceau for France) who were wily political operators. He did not press the Italian case effectively in the face of such opposition.

## Complete the paragraph

Below are a sample exam-style question and a paragraph written in answer to this question. The paragraph contains a point and specific examples, but lacks a concluding explanatory link back to the question. Complete the paragraph adding this link in the space provided.

How far does Italy's 'mutilated victory' after the First World War account for the weaknesses of the Liberal State in the period 1918–22?

> Italy's 'mutilated victory' after the First World War played an important role in weakening the Liberal State in the period 1918–22. In Italy, there was widespread disappointment with the Treaty of St Germain. For example, the Italian negotiators had demanded that Italy share in the redistribution of colonies belonging to Germany and Turkey. However, this demand was refused. In addition, Italian negotiators had asked for the port of Fiume and parts of Dalmatia. This request was also refused, and these territories were given to Yugoslavia. Many in Italy believed that these terms were insulting to Italy and did not reflect Italy's role in the war.
>
> _____
>
> _____

## Identify an argument

Below are a series of definitions, a sample exam-style question and two sample conclusions. One of the conclusions achieves a high level because it contains an argument. The other achieves a lower level because it is contains only description and assertion. Identify which is which. The mark scheme on page 3 will help you.

- Description: a detailed account.
- Assertion: a statement of fact or an opinion which is not supported by a reason.
- Reason: a statement which explains or justifies something.
- Argument: an assertion justified with a reason.

How far does Italy's 'mutilated victory' after the First World War account for increasing dissatisfaction with the Liberal government in Italy in the period 1918–22?

### Sample 1

> Overall, Italy's 'mutilated victory' played a key role in accounting for increasing dissatisfaction with the Liberal government in Italy in the period 1918–22. Many Italians were unhappy with the terms of the Treaty of St Germain and believed that the Liberal government had failed to ensure that Italy was justly rewarded for its role in the war. Consequently, while other factors, such as economic problems and social problems, heightened tensions, the impact of the 'mutilated victory' was most important because it created the impression that the Italian government was not acting in the interests of the Italian people.

### Sample 2

> Overall, Italy's 'mutilated victory' played a role in accounting for increasing dissatisfaction with the Liberal government in Italy in the period 1918–22. The terms of the Treaty of St Germain did not reflect the demands of Italian nationalists, and many people were disappointed with the peace settlement. However, the terms of the Treaty reflected the fact that Britain and France had contributed more to the war in terms of people and resources. In addition, the Italian negotiators did not make their demands strongly, and so many of their requests were overlooked.

## The political impact of the war

The war had long-lasting political and social consequences which created problems for the Liberal State. Existing divisions deepened, undermining democracy.

### Political divisions

Prime Minister Antonio Salandra hoped that war would unite the nation, but entry into the war was **divisive**. At the outbreak of war the majority of the population was against it. Liberals tended to argue that there was no national interest in joining the war. Most Catholics supported neutrality and most socialists argued for pacifism.

Some did welcome the war. Radicals, and a minority of socialists like **Benito Mussolini**, believed that the war would lead to revolution across Europe. Nationalists wanted to expand Italy's **sphere of influence** by beating the **Central Powers**. Nonetheless, there was little unity between these groups because their reasons for supporting the war were so different.

Salandra believed the war would be short and Italy's victory would win over the majority of the people.

### War and democracy

The war eroded Italian democracy in several ways:

- Salandra ruled by decree, therefore the democratically elected parliament lost its power to make laws.
- Salandra rarely allowed parliament to meet, as he wanted to minimise public criticism of his polices.
- Unelected military leaders grew in power as the government prioritised military requirements to win the war.
- Public confidence in democracy was weakened as many felt that the democratic parliament had failed to stop the war.
- Traditional party politics were weakened by splits over issues such as entering the war, and whether Italy should continue fighting.
- The Liberals were discredited for failing to win a better deal for Italy at the Paris Peace Conference.
- The war created greater pressure for democratic reform.

### Democratic reforms

Following the war, radical democratic reforms were introduced. The reforms were put in place in time for the November 1919 elections:

- **Universal male suffrage** was introduced.
- The **electoral system** was changed with the introduction of the **party list system**.

### The impact of reform

The reforms further destabilised Italian democracy by undermining the established political parties.

- The war undermined the power of the alliance between Italian liberals and the traditional elites. At the same time, new mass political parties started to become more powerful. Following the war, therefore, groups with mass appeal were likely to win power.
- The Liberal Party lacked cohesion, discipline and organisation – the reforms showed that political parties now needed to garner mass public support rather than rely on links with the traditional elites.
- The Socialist parties had access to the mass audiences necessary to gain support, but they refused to take part in coalition government in order to undermine parliamentary democracy.
- The Catholic Popular Party (PPI) – this party was created in 1919 after Pope Benedict XV gave Catholics permission to participate in national elections. The liberals needed to form coalitions with the PPI if the Socialists would not do so, but the liberals and the PPI had little in common. This led to frequent crises as **anti-clerical** liberals would not compromise with PPI demands on issues such as education and female suffrage.

The failure of these parties to work together caused the erosion of public confidence in the parliamentary systems. Together, the impact of the war and the reforms led to widespread disenchantment with the Liberal State.

Below are a sample exam-style question and a paragraph written in answer to this question. Why does this paragraph not get into Level 4? Once you have identified the mistake, rewrite the paragraph so that it displays the qualities of Level 4. The mark scheme on page 3 will help you.

To what extent were the democratic reforms of 1919 responsible for the political instability of the Liberal State in the years 1896–1922?

> The democratic reforms of 1919 were partially responsible for the political instability of the Liberal State in the years 1896–1922. The reforms introduced universal male suffrage and changed the electoral system. These were radical changes and they came into force in time for the November 1919 elections. The changes led to widespread dissatisfaction with the Liberal government.

 Develop the detail    **a**

Below are a sample exam-style 24 mark question and a paragraph written in answer to this question. The paragraph contains a limited amount of detail. Annotate the paragraph to add additional detail to the answer.

How far was Italy's involvement in the First World War the main reason for the collapse of the Liberal State?

> One way in which Italy's involvement in the First World War contributed to the collapse of the Liberal State was that the war weakened confidence in Italian democracy. For example, the Prime Minister rarely allowed Parliament to meet. In addition, as a result of the war, many unelected leaders became more powerful. Consequently, the war created pressure for political reform, and radical democratic reforms were introduced. However, these reforms created further political problems. In this way, Italy's involvement in the First World War highlighted the weaknesses of Italian democracy and led to widespread disenchantment with the Liberal State.

## The economic impact of the war

The war economy succeeded in supplying the army. However, its political effects were devastating, as it led to economic chaos and the threat of revolution.

### Creating a war economy

Before the war, many people were afraid that a long conflict would shatter the economy. In this context the success of the Italian war economy appeared to be an 'economic miracle'. The Italian government achieved this by establishing an **Undersecretariat of Arms and Munitions** which offered cheap loans, payment in advance and lucrative contracts to favoured companies. The companies that benefited from the war economy included:

- Fiat – the car manufacturer
- Montecatini – a chemicals company
- Breda – engineering specialists.

### The political consequences of the war economy

The war economy weakened Italian democracy. Essentially, the economy was controlled by committees of military leaders and senior businessmen, or government **technocrats** who were not accountable to the people or parliament.

Additionally, the government failed to control business during the war, so businesses could keep wages low and raise the price of their goods. Consequently, the authority of the government was weakened because many workers and peasants believed that the government was on the side of big business rather than ordinary people.

### The economic consequences of the war economy

The war economy created post-war problems that further undermined the Liberal State:

- Economic growth during the war had depended on state spending so, once the war was over, major businesses suffered because a major source of income stopped. Demand fell steeply and **share prices** halved. Two major munitions companies, Ansaldo and Ilva, collapsed in 1921.
- Wartime spending led to a severe **budget deficit** – Italy spent approximately 41 billion lire during the war, and owed 23.3 billion after the war.
- The government printed money to help pay back British and American war loans. This led to **inflation**. By 1920, the lira was worth only 25 per cent of its value in 1914. The cost of living quadrupled in the same time. Inflation hit the value of savings, pensions and real wages.

### The war economy and the Liberal State

The war economy weakened the Liberal State in several ways:

- It led to a post-war economic crisis which created massive industrial unrest.
- Italian workers and peasants blamed the government for the economic crisis and began campaigning for more radical alternatives.
- Middle-class Italians feared that the Liberal State was unable to control the workers and therefore they started supporting more radical anti-socialist alternatives.
- The war economy created a network of powerful unelected economic managers who refused to give up their power once the war was over.

Below are a sample exam-style question and a paragraph written in answer to this question. Read the paragraph and the mark scheme provided on page 3. Decide which level you would award the paragraph. Write the level below, along with a justification for your choice.

How far was the economic impact of the First World War the main reason for the collapse of the Liberal State?

The economic impact of the First World War was an important reason for the collapse of the Liberal State. For example, the government did not control business practices during the war, allowing businesses to raise prices and keep wages low. This gave the impression that the government cared more about the interests of business than the interests of the workers and peasants. Consequently, the workers and peasants turned against the government and began to support more radical political parties. In addition, the war was followed by economic crisis. For example, by 1920, the lira was worth only 20 per cent of its value in 1914. This crisis led to industrial unrest which alienated the middle class, who began to support political parties who opposed socialism. In this way, the economic impact of the First World War played an important role in decreasing support for the Liberal State, and increasing support for parties that opposed the government.

Level:          Reason for choosing this level:

_____

Below are a sample exam-style question and a series of assertions. Read the exam question and then add a justification to each of the assertions to turn it into an argument.

How far was the economic impact of the First World War the main reason for the collapse of the Liberal State?

The relationship between the government and big business during the war contributed to the collapse of the Liberal State because

_____

The post-war economic crisis contributed to the collapse of the liberal state because

_____

Industrial unrest following the First World War contributed to the collapse of the Liberal State because

_____

## The social impact of the war

The First World War, and its aftermath, led to growing unrest among Italian workers and peasants.

### Workers and peasants

The First World War was socially divisive because it aggravated existing social tensions.

- During the War, the North–South divide became deeper. The war economy (see page 22) led to prosperity in modern industrial cities like Turin, but there was little economic growth in rural areas. This emphasised the economic underdevelopment of the Italian country.

- **Land hunger** increased among the peasants due to the hope that more land would be available after the war. Therefore peasants started seizing land in 1918.

- The war economy prioritised military production over food. Consequently, there were food shortages during the war that caused resentment amongst the working class.

- Workers resented new labour laws which outlawed strikes, led to much longer hours (one company had a 75-hour week) and subjected workers to military courts. Increasing numbers of workers joined Socialist trade unions, and the number of strikes increased. In 1919 over 1 million workers took part in strikes.

- Workers denounced big businesses that made huge profits out of wartime contracts. They argued that these **profiteers** used the war to their advantage while the poor made real sacrifices for the nation.

- The government refused to pay for the war out of **progressive taxation**. Rather they increased **indirect taxation**. This had a much greater impact on the poor, and caused outrage among Italy's Socialists.

### Soldiers

The war led many soldiers to turn against the government as:

- For several years the Italian army achieved little. Many soldiers blamed the government for forcing them to take part in 'useless slaughter'. Indeed, by 1916 discontent led to **mutinies**.

- Soldiers resented the harsh military discipline. 4000 Italian soldiers were sentenced to death by military courts, the highest number of any of the Entente armies.

- Soldiers who had returned from frontline fighting bitterly resented workers who were exempted from military service. Soldiers saw these workers as cowards and **shirkers**. This led to divisions within communities, which worsened as returning soldiers found it hard to get jobs.

### Industrial unrest

The economic impact of the war continued to cause conflict after fighting had ceased. Post-war inflation and unemployment led to unrest:

- The workforce became increasingly militant. Between 1918 and 1920, trade union membership increased from 250,000 to 2 million, with more than 1.2 million workers in Catholic rather than socialist trade unions.

- Economic problems, a loss of trust in the government, and post-war unemployment led to growing numbers of strikes:

| Year | Number of striking workers | Number of strikes |
|------|----------------------------|-------------------|
| 1914 | 170,000 | 781 |
| 1919 | 1.5 million | 1,860 |

Working-class radicalism caused many in the middle class to fear that a revolution was imminent. Indeed, working-class protest was so widespread that the period 1918–19 became known as 'the red years'.

### Summary

Overall, the war proved divisive. The war economy increased existing tensions by helping the development of the cities at the expense of the country, and by subjecting workers to harsh conditions while big businesses made huge profits. The government's failure to make significant territorial gains and continuing economic problems after the war further destabilised Italy's Liberal State.

## Spectrum of significance

Below are a sample exam-style question and a list of general points which could be used to answer the question. Use your own knowledge and the information on the opposite page to reach a judgement about the importance of these general points to the question posed. Write numbers on the spectrum below to indicate their relative importance. Having done this, write a brief justification of your placement, explaining why some of these factors are more important than others. The resulting diagram could form the basis of an essay plan.

How far do you agree that the impact of the First World War on Italian society was the main reason for the collapse of the Liberal State?

1. The impact of the war on Italian society
2. The impact of the 'mutilated victory'
3. The political impact of the war
4. The democratic reforms of 1919
5. The economic impact of the war

Less important                                           Very important

## Complex essay style

Below are a sample exam-style question, a list of key points to be made in the essay, and a simple introduction and conclusion for the essay. Read the question, the plan, and the introduction and conclusion. Rewrite the introduction and the conclusion in order to develop an argument.

How far do you agree that the impact of the First World War on Italian society was the main reason for the weaknesses in the Liberal State in the period 1918–22?

### Key points

- The impact of the war on Italian society
- The impact of the 'mutilated victory'
- The political impact of the war
- The democratic reforms of 1919
- The economic impact of the war

### Introduction

> There were five key reasons why the Liberal State was weak in the period 1918–22. These were the impact of the war on Italian society, the impact of the 'mutilated victory', the political impact of the war, the democratic reforms of 1919, and the economic impact of the war.

### Conclusion

> There were five key reasons why the Liberal State was weak in the period 1918–22. The most important reason was the economic impact of the war. This played a more significant role than all of the other factors.

## D'Annunzio's Fiume

### What happened at Fiume in September 1919?

At the end of the First World War, Italian nationalists demanded the Adriatic port Fiume as part of the peace settlement (see page 18) but it was instead given to the newly created Yugoslavia. In September 1919 around 2000 Italian soldiers, led by the nationalist Gabriele D'Annunzio, seized it. The soldiers were mostly mutineers and deserters who nationalists, senior army officers and sympathetic conservative industrialists had organised for the seizure. The seizure was in defiance of the Italian government and reveals just how angry and betrayed the Italian military felt about the Treaty of St Germain.

### D'Annunzio's success

The invasion of Fiume succeeded so easily because the commander of the local Italian troops, General Pittaluga, refused to stop D'Annunzio's soldiers. Italians living in Fiume welcomed the occupiers as 'liberators'. Against the wishes of the Italian government, Yugoslavia and the Western powers, Fiume was held for over a year. The occupation was also very popular in the rest of Italy, where D'Annunzio was seen as a hero because he had succeeded where the Italian government had failed.

### Fiume under D'Annunzio

D'Annunzio declared Fiume an independent republic and himself 'Regent'. He took over the Governor's Palace of Fiume for his headquarters, organised rallies and nationalist ceremonies, and announced a constitution for the republic. A newspaper was founded and a local militia established to defend the new 'state'. D'Annunzio hoped that this was just the beginning and that Fiume would be his base to march on Rome.

Orlando, the Liberal Prime Minister and negotiator at the Paris peace conference, resigned in June 1919. The new government, headed by Francesco Nitti, did not use the army against D'Annunzio's forces because of the popularity of the occupation. This helped the occupation to last for so long.

### How was the situation resolved?

Giolitti (see page 14) became Prime Minister again in June 1920. He took a much firmer stance in relation to Fiume. Instead of dealing with D'Annunzio, he negotiated with Yugoslavia and agreed the Treaty of Rapallo with them in November 1920.

Under the Treaty:

- Italian speakers in Dalmatia could choose to become Italian citizens.
- Fiume was made an independent city under international control.

D'Annunzio, however, refused to accept the Treaty. Consequently, in December 1920 Italy declared war on Fiume. An Italian battleship shelled D'Annunzio's palace and troops stormed the port. D'Annunzio and his 'legionaries' surrendered after four days of fighting in which 52 people died.

D'Annunzio was never put on trial for his actions in Fiume because the Italian government wanted to avoid the publicity that trying this popular figure would bring.

### Fiume's significance

- The popularity of the seizure of Fiume showed just how dissatisfied Italians were with the post-war Treaty of St Germain.
- It revealed weaknesses in the Italian state, especially that the government could not rely on the army's loyalty.
- It demonstrated that direct action could be more effective than Italy's traditional political methods of compromise and negotiation.
- D'Annunzio developed a new style of mass politics – balcony speeches, the '**Roman salute**', chanting slogans and humiliating opponents by forcing them to drink castor oil. This heavily influenced Benito Mussolini after he visited Fiume during the occupation.

## Support or challenge?

Below is a sample exam-style question which asks how far you agree with a specific statement. Below this are a series of general statements which are relevant to the question. Using your own knowledge and the information on the opposite page decide whether these statements support or challenge the statement in the question and tick the appropriate box.

'The invasion of Fiume in 1919 weakened the Liberal State in Italy.' How far do you agree with this statement?

|  | Support | Challenge |
|---|---|---|
| The invasion occurred in defiance of the Italian government. |  |  |
| Two thousand soldiers were involved in the seizure. |  |  |
| The invasion was very popular with the Italian public. |  |  |
| Giolitti and Yugoslavia signed the Treaty of Rapallo. |  |  |
| D'Annunzio was forced to end his occupation after Italian troops attacked Fiume. | ` |  |
| D'Annunzio was never put on trial. |  |  |

## Eliminate irrelevance

Below are a sample exam-style question and a paragraph written in answer to this question. Read the paragraph and identify parts of the paragraph that are not directly relevant to the question. Draw a line through the information that is irrelevant and justify your deletions in the margin.

How far do you agree that the invasion of Fiume was the main reason for the political instability of the Liberal State in the years 1918–22?

The invasion of Fiume in September 1919 played a key role in undermining the Liberal State in the years 1918–22. In this respect, the invasion was significant for three reasons. Firstly, the invasion showed the lack of support for the government among the military. The invasion, which involved two thousand soldiers, occurred in defiance of the Liberal government, and indicated that many in the military were not loyal to the government. This had also been a problem in 1916, when many soldiers had mutinied in protest at Italian involvement in the First World War. Secondly, the invasion showed the lack of popular support for the Liberal government. Many in Italy supported the invasion, and viewed D'Annunzio as a hero. D'Annunzio was also famous for coming up with the term 'mutilated victory' to describe the view that Italy had been treated badly in the negotiations following the First World War. Thirdly, the invasion demonstrated the power of direct action, undermining the Liberal State's reliance on compromise and negotiation. In this way, the invasion of Fiume contributed to the political instability of the Liberal State in the years 1918–22 by emphasising the level of popular dissatisfaction with the Liberal government and their methods.

## The emergence of Fascism

In 1919 Fascist groups emerged, advocating radical change. Three years later, after widespread political unrest, Fascist leader Mussolini was appointed as Prime Minister.

### Why was Fascism popular?

Following the First World War, Fascism offered a radical alternative to traditional politics:

- Many believed that the 'mutilated victory' showed that traditional political parties had failed the nation. They felt that Fiume showed that radical new nationalist movements could succeed where old politicians had failed.
- Nationalists believed that the army had achieved great things during the First World War, therefore they believed that military organisation and military tactics were superior to traditional politics. The **squadristi** and the National Fascist Party (PNF) were modelled on the Army, so many people believed Fascism would achieve more than traditional political parties.
- Unlike traditional politicians, the Fascists effectively resisted socialism and the trade unions.

### The emergence of Fascism, 1919–22

#### The *squadristi*

The *squadristi* or 'blackshirts' were local **militia** groups that emerged after the First World War. They were largely made up of demobilised soldiers and middle class young people who were disillusioned with traditional politics. The *squadristi* were modelled on the army's elite troops, and funded by big landowners and businesses who relied on them to crush rebellious workers and peasants. Indeed, Mussolini described *squadristi* violence as a 'guerrilla war' against socialism.

#### A national organisation

In February 1919 Mussolini turned the local groups of *squadristi*, as well as other nationalist radicals, into a national movement: the *Fasci di Combattimento*. Their manifesto, published in June, called for:

- the abolition of the monarchy
- universal suffrage

- confiscation of war profits
- an eight-hour working day
- Italy to take Fiume and Dalmatia.

Between 1919 and 1921, the *Fasci di Combattimento* emerged as a popular new political movement.

### Mussolini's pact with Giolitti

Giolitti formed an alliance with the PNF ahead of the May 1921 election. His negotiations with Mussolini led to a formal agreement to stand together as a 'National Block'. Giolitti created the alliance for several reasons:

- He believed that it would stop the PNF becoming a greater threat.
- He also saw them as a useful ally against the Socialists in the May 1921elections.

The Fascists gained 35 seats in the elections – including one for Mussolini. Once the National Block had served Mussolini's purpose, he broke off his alliance with Giolitti. The alliance gave Mussolini greater authority, a respectable image and a foothold on legitimate power. Giolitti, having greatly underestimated the Fascists, resigned in June 1921 when the coalition collapsed.

### Pact with the Socialists

Prior to his resignation, Giolitti attempted to end political violence by negotiating the Pact of Pacification. The Pact, signed by the Socialists and the Fascists, required both sides to stop violence. However, the Pact was short-lived, and violence restarted in November 1921.

Nonetheless, the Pact caused problems within the Fascist movement. Many Fascist leaders opposed the pact as they feared it would undermine the *squadristi*. Consequently, Mussolini resigned from the Fascist executive in August and senior Fascists offered D'Annunzio the party leadership at a meeting at Bologna.

Ultimately, Mussolini remained leader because D'Annunzio turned down the leadership, and because the majority of leading Fascists supported the Pact.

Complete these activities once you have read this topic (page 28) and the next topic (page 30).

 RAG – Rate the timeline

Below are a sample exam-style question and a timeline. Read the question, study the timeline and, using three coloured pens, put a red, amber or green star next to the events to show:

- red – events and policies that have no relevance to the question
- amber – events and policies that have some significance to the question
- green – events and policies that are directly relevant to the question.

1) To what extent was Mussolini responsible for the growing power of Fascism in Italy in the period 1919–22?

Now repeat the activity with the following questions:

2) How far does Italy's 'mutilated victory' after the First World War account for the weaknesses of the Liberal State in the period 1918–22?

3) How accurate is it to say that the Italian Liberal State was responsible for its own downfall?

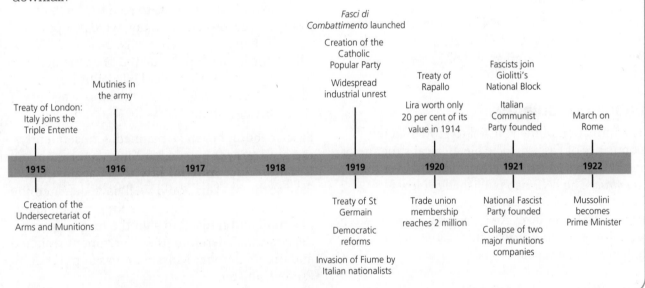

 Simple essay style

Above are three sample exam-style questions. Use your own knowledge and the information in this section to produce plans for each question. Choose four general points, and provide three pieces of specific information to support each general point. Once you have planned each essay, write the introduction and conclusion for the essay. The introduction should list the points to be discussed in the essay. The conclusion should summarise the key points and justify which point was the most important.

## The March on Rome

### Mussolini's new strategy

The failure of the Pact of Pacification, led Mussolini to reverse his strategy. Rather than compromise, he praised the *squadristi*. He now aimed to gain control by creating a national political party.

### The National Fascist Party (PNF)

Mussolini formally renounced the Pact of Pacification in November 1921, a week after the National Fascist Party (PNF). The timing was tactical, as once Mussolini rejected the Pact, Prime Minister Ivanoe Bonomi banned all armed organisations. However, he was not prepared to ban the Fascist Party outright, as the Party was growing in popularity and as it was technically separate from the violent *squadristi*.

By December 1921, the PNF had grown to 218,000 members and 1333 *fasci*. This was a huge increase from the 80,476 members and 371 *fasci* of May 1921.

### Fascist popularity

The formation of the PNF led to growth in the popularity of Fascism. The hierarchical structure of the PNF gave Mussolini greater control over the *squadristi*. The PNF also published a 'New Programme' which gained support from the elite by promising lower taxes for business and farmers. The promise of compulsory military service also appealed to nationalists.

### Growing fascist power

Local fascist groups began forcibly ejecting elected authorities in early 1922. They took control of these areas, dominating local government, levying unofficial taxes and using the **syndicates** to control the job market. Left-wing protests against this were used by Mussolini as propaganda opportunities – he claimed that the Fascists were restoring and maintaining order.

### Mussolini's relationship with the elites

While encouraging the PNF's direct action, Mussolini knew he had to restrain the squads' violence to prevent an armed state intervention. He allayed Liberal suspicion by negotiating with them and presenting himself as someone who could discipline those Fascists who went too far.

Mussolini cultivated the support of senior army officials and attempted to win over the King, Victor Emmanuel III. The King could order an armed response to the Fascists and also appointed the Prime Minister.

### Mussolini becomes Prime Minister

On 16 October 1922, Mussolini met with PNF leaders and senior Fascists to plan a 'March on Rome'. Decisions about timing were postponed until the party's conference in Naples on 24 October. There, the leadership decided to seize the northern and central cities not under PNF control from midnight on 27 October and then move against Rome the day after.

Fascist action began as planned. Consequently, the government persuaded King Victor Emmanuel II to introduce **martial law** to act against the Fascist threat. This could well have defeated the movement but, by 9a.m., the King had changed his mind and refused to sign the martial law declaration. Therefore, the government resigned and on 30 October Mussolini was appointed Prime Minister.

---

### Why was Mussolini appointed Prime Minister?

- The government's resignation meant that a new coalition needed to be formed – which, due to the necessities of *trasformismo*, was always difficult.
- The liberals were divided and therefore weak. When the King asked Salandra to form a new government, liberal in-fighting meant that many liberals refused to support him.
- Salandra suggested that the King send for Mussolini in order to thwart his rival Giolitti.
- Mussolini refused to support any government unless he was made Prime Minister.

Spectrum of significance

Below is a sample exam-style question and a list of general points which could be used to answer the question. Use your own knowledge and the information on the opposite page to reach a judgement about the importance of these general points to the question posed. Write numbers on the spectrum below to indicate their relative importance. Having done this, write a brief justification of your placement, explaining why some of these factors are more important than others. The resulting diagram could form the basis of an essay plan.

Why, in October 1922, was Mussolini appointed Prime Minister?

1. The economic impact of the First World War
2. The impact of the 'mutilated victory'
3. Political divisions
4. Social problems
5. The impact of the invasion of Fiume
6. The organisation and policies of Italian Fascists
7. The actions of Mussolini

Less important                                                       Very important

 Complex essay style

Below are a sample exam-style question, a list of key points to be made in the essay, and a simple introduction and conclusion for the essay. Read the question, the plan, and the introduction and conclusion. Rewrite the introduction and the conclusion in order to develop an argument.

Why, in October 1922, was Mussolini appointed Prime Minister?

**Key points**

- The economic impact of the First World War
- The impact of the 'mutilated victory'
- Political divisions
- Social problems
- The impact of the invasion of Fiume
- The organisation and policies of Italian Fascists
- The actions of Mussolini

### Introduction

There were seven key reasons Mussolini was appointed Prime Minister in October 1922. These were the economic impact of the First World War, the impact of the 'mutilated victory', political divisions, social problems, the impact of the invasion of Fiume, the organisation and policies of Italian Fascists, and the actions of Mussolini.

### Conclusion

There were seven key reasons Mussolini was appointed Prime Minister in October 1922. The most important reason was the actions of Mussolini. This played a more significant role than all of the other factors.

## The appeal of Fascism 1919–22

Fascism attracted support from many social groups. One of the reasons for this was that the PNF was not completely united and its ideology was inconsistent. This meant that the PNF could offer different things to different groups.

### Who were the Fascist supporters?

The *Fasci* movement emerged in 1919 and had very few members – at best, a few thousand. Their early supporters were middle-class students and demobilised soldiers, often former army officers and from the junior ranks. Their aim was to re-establish Italy as a Great Power. For young people, Fascism seemed to be an exciting new movement that would help Italy achieve what it had failed to achieve in the 'mutilated victory'.

### Rural supporters

New recruits from 1920 included:

- **Sharecroppers**
- Small farmers
- Farm managers.

They were the wealthier peasants who wanted to buy their own land, and were frightened and angered by the Socialist ideas of land **collectivisation** and higher wage rates. They took part in Fascist violence or funded the Fascist squads in their campaigns.

### Urban supporters

A significant source of Fascist support in the towns was the lower middle class. They blamed the government for high inflation, unemployment and the growth of socialism. They included office workers, teachers, shopkeepers and other small business owners, and were mostly young. Fascism seemed an exciting and dynamic movement, very different from the cynical politics of *trasformismo*. Around 10 per cent of Fascist members were students and 25 per cent were too young to vote.

Some urban workers were also attracted to Fascism, mainly because of the very radical elements to the Fascist manifesto like the eight-hour day, fair wages and prices, and employee representatives in management positions. Some of these urban workers also hated the socialist intimidation of non-unionised workforces. They began to take over former socialist areas. This led to more workers joining the local Fascist syndicates so that they could get jobs.

### Elite support

The PNF also gained a great deal of support from Italy's elite. Industrialists had become increasingly disillusioned with Liberal politics as they blamed the government for doing too little to control the workers. They were anxious that democracy would lead to the rise of socialism and therefore increased power for workers. Consequently, many supported the PNF which was anti-democratic and committed to fighting socialism. Indeed, elite groups began to turn to local Fascist groups by the end of 1920. One of the earliest examples of this was in Bologna, in November 1920, where the Fascists attacked the inauguration of the new Socialist council.

Local Fascist groups, though small in size, carried out attacks which included burning down Socialist offices, beating up trade unionists and forcing opponents to drink castor oil (a method pioneered by D'Annunzio – see page 26).

### The middle class

Like the elites, the middle class were frightened by the growing power of the working class. Consequently, they too supported the PNF in order to prevent socialism gaining power. Additionally, many in the middle class believed that recent history had shown democracy was inferior to expert government. The war economy, they argued, was successful because it was controlled by experts. Italy's democratically elected governments following the First World War had failed to control the socialists or generate economic growth. Many in the middle class supported the PNF as they believed that they would end democracy and return power to middle class experts.

## Spider diagram

Use the information on the opposite page to add detail to the spider diagram below.

```
                    ┌─────────────────────┐
   ┌──────────────┐ │   Why did people    │ ┌──────────────┐
   │ Dissatisfaction │ support the Fascists │ │ The appeal of │
   │   with        │─│   in the period     │─│ Fascist policies │
   │ the Liberal State │ │     1919–22?      │ │              │
   └──────────────┘ └─────────────────────┘ └──────────────┘
```

## Simple essay style

Below are two sample exam-style questions. Use your own knowledge and the information in this section to produce a plan for each of these questions. Choose four general points, and provide three pieces of specific information to support each general point. Once you have planned each essay, write the introduction and conclusion for the essay. The introduction should list the points to be discussed in the essay. The conclusion should summarise the key points and justify which point was the most important.

How far do you agree that Fascist economic policies were responsible for the growing support for the Italian Fascist Party in the years 1919–22?

How far does the growth of the Italian Fascist Party explain the collapse of the Liberal State in Italy?

## Recommended reading

Below is a list of suggested further reading on this topic.

- *Italy: The Rise of Fascism 1915–1945*, chapter 3, Mark Robson (2006)
- *Fascist Italy*, chapters 1 and 2, John Whittam (1995)
- *Mussolini and Italy*, pages 149–159, Edward Townley (2002)

## Exam focus

Below is a sample A grade essay. Read it and the comments around it.

How far does Italy's 'mutilated victory' explain growing support for the Italian Fascist Party in the years 1919–22?

The introduction indicates that the essay will discuss four major factors. It asserts that the First World War was the most important factor, but it does not support this with an argument or with evidence.

Italy's 'mutilated victory' was clearly one reason for the growing support for the Italian Fascist Party in the years immediately following the First World War. However, the most important reason was the war itself. Other factors included the radical example of D'Annunzio and the appeal of Fascism.

The first sentence of the paragraph contains a clear link to the question, suggesting that the paragraph will be focused on the question.

Italy's 'mutilated victory' certainly led to growing support for the Italian Fascist Party. At the end of the First World War Italy failed to gain the territory that many nationalists thought it deserved. Having won the war, Italy demanded, new territory including the port of Fiume, South Tyrol, the Trentino, Istria, parts of Dalmatia and overseas colonies that had once belonged to Turkey. However, except for South Tyrol, Trentino and Istria, the Italian government failed to gain these territories in negotiations over the 1919 Treaty of St Germain. This failure, which the radical nationalist poet D'Annunzio called the 'mutilated victory', led many Italians to believe that the Liberal State and traditional politicians had failed Italy. The 'mutilated victory' led to growing support for the Italian Fascist Party because many radical nationalists felt that, unlike traditional politicians, the Fascists would always put Italy first.

However, the First World War was the main reason for the growth in support for the Fascist Party in 1919–22. The First World War had many consequences for Italian politics. First, during the war Italian democracy was eroded. The war led to a growth in the power of the Prime Minister, and a reduction in the power of Parliament. Also it led to the growth in power of unelected Military leaders. Fascists would later argue that the success of Italy's war effort proved that these undemocratic methods were more effective than democratic methods. Also the war led to discontent. Workers and peasants were angry that they worked hard to support the war effort, but big business profited. Indeed, workers had to work a 75-hour week. Soldiers were also angry at profiteers who had made money while they fought. Soldiers also objected to the workers who went on strike during the war. The war led to a growth in support for the Fascists because they represented a group who were prepared to continue using undemocratic methods and a group who wanted the whole nation to sacrifice for the common good rather than allowing some groups to shirk their responsibilities or make profit at the expense of the nation.

The last sentence of the paragraph clearly explains how changes brought about by the First World War led to growing support for Fascism.

D'Annunzio's occupation of Fiume also led to the rise of Fascism. To many nationalists, D'Annunzio seemed to be a new type of politician. D'Annunzio became a national hero during the First World War for his heroics as a soldier. In September 1919 he led around 2,000 Italian soldiers into Fiume, and took by force what Italian politicians had failed to gain by negotiation. Whilst in power in Fiume, D'Annunzio organised a new radical kind of nationalist politics which made use of theatrical ceremonies and parades. For many nationalists this was an attractive alternative to traditional Italian politics. Whereas traditional politicians had failed Italy in their negotiations, D'Annunzio used force to take what he felt Italy deserved. D'Annunzio's actions in Fiume helped increase support for Fascism because the Fascists seemed to offer Italy an effective, heroic and radical alternative to traditional politics, just like D'Annunzio had offered Fiume.

This paragraph effectively contrasts the apparent failure of traditional politics with the apparent success of D'Annunzio's radical alternative. It concludes by linking this to Fascism.

As well as the failings of traditional politics, Fascism was also attractive to many Italians. Many nationalists respected Fasci di Combattimento. These groups were made up of heroic ex-soldiers who had fought bravely for Italy. Unlike traditional politicians they had achieved a true victory rather than letting Italy down through failed negotiations. Also the squadristi were attractive because they functioned more like an army than like a traditional political party. Again, this appealed to many who felt the army had succeeded where traditional politics had failed. Also the squadristi fought an effective 'guerrilla war' against socialism. Again standing up to socialists in a way that traditional politicians like Giolitti had failed to. Finally, Mussolini's promises to subordinate individual freedoms to the national interest as part of his radical nationalist 'New Programme' of 1921 persuaded many nationalists that the Fascists were a dynamic new force who could lead the nation where traditional leaders had failed.

This paragraph uses technical terms such as *squadristi* and specific dates to increase the level of detail used in the essay.

In conclusion, Italy's 'mutilated victory' was only one reason for the growing support for the Italian Fascist Party. However, other factors included the impact of the First World War and the radicalism of D'Annunzio, the squadristi and Mussolini's 1921 'New Programme' also played a part in the growth of support for the Italian Fascist Party in the years 1919–22.

This paragraph summarised the rest of the essay, but does not give an overall argument.

24/30

This is a well-focused essay which includes a large amount of relevant detail. Every paragraph presents a coherent analysis of the factor it discusses. Nonetheless, this essay cannot enter Level 5 because the introduction and conclusion simply summarise the essay and there is no attempt to develop an overall argument. Indeed, while the essay asserts that the war was the most important factor, it does not put forward an argument to prove this.

## Moving from Level 4 to Level 5

The Exam Focus at the end of Section 1 provided a Level 5 essay. The essay here achieves a Level 4. Read both essays, and the examiner's comments provided. Make a list of the additional features required to push a Level 4 essay into Level 5.

# Section 3:
# Power and control in Fascist Italy

## Mussolini's position in 1922

In 1922 Mussolini was Italy's Prime Minister, head of a coalition government. However, he was still a long way from total power. The obstacles to a Fascist dictatorship included:

- other political parties
- independent trades unions
- regular democratic elections
- civil rights
- conservative and liberal aspirations to 'tame' Fascism.

Nonetheless, radical Fascists wanted Mussolini to transform Italy into a Fascist state. Between 1922 and 1925 Mussolini moved slowly towards dictatorship.

## Emergency powers

Mussolini's first step was to gain emergency powers. In November 1922, shortly after becoming Prime Minister, Mussolini demanded that parliament grant him the power to **rule by decree** in order to restore law and order. Mussolini's coalition partners agreed, and Mussolini was granted emergency power for twelve months. Consequently, Mussolini was able to pass laws, without consulting parliament, for most of 1923.

## Key appointments

Mussolini also strengthened his position by appointing Fascists to key positions in government. Mussolini took control of the **Foreign Ministry** and the **Ministry of the Interior**. He appointed the pro-Fascist **Alberto De Stefani** as finance minister, and the Fascist **Emilio De Bono** as head of the police. Finally, he appointed loyal Fascists as under-secretaries in most government ministries.

As well as appointing his own supporters, Mussolini appointed liberals and conservatives to key positions to give the appearance of moderation. In this way he could appease liberals and conservatives. Indeed, his first Cabinet included four liberals, two populists and nationalists, as well as four members of the PNF.

## Controlling Fascism

Since 1919 Fascist organisations had proved difficult to control. Mussolini brought the Fascist movement under his control during the early 1920s in two ways. First, in December 1922, he created the Grand Council of Fascism, made up of leading members of the PNF. Mussolini used it to dominate other leading Fascists, and therefore extend his control over the party.

Second, he disciplined the *squadristi* by creating an official state-funded Fascist Militia (MSVN). It was controlled by ex-army officers and limited to 300,000 members all of whom swore an oath of loyalty to Mussolini. The Grand Council and the MSVN gave its members a higher status within the movement and therefore Mussolini gained the loyalty of Fascists at all levels of the movement. As well as disciplining the Black Shirts, the MSVN gave Mussolini a powerful private army, thus weakening the Army's position and making an anti-Fascist **military coup** less likely.

## The cheka

Mussolini also established a personal bodyguard, known as the **cheka**, which protected him and intimidated his political opponents. Indeed, **Ameriqo Dumini**, the cheka's leader, played a key role in the murder of Giacomo Matteotti (see page 38).

## The electoral law

To guarantee strong government, Giacomo Acerbo, a Fascist sympathiser and parliamentary deputy, proposed a reform to the election laws. Acerbo proposed that the most popular party in an election should gain two-thirds of the seats in parliament. The remaining third would then be divided among the other parties according to the proportion of votes they received. This, he argued, would end the need for coalitions and ensure strong government. The law, which became known as the Acerbo Law, was passed in November 1923.

**Support or challenge?**

Below is a sample exam-style question which asks how far you agree with a specific statement. Below this are a series of general statements which are relevant to the question. Using your own knowledge and the information on the opposite page, decide whether these statements support or challenge the statement in the question and tick the appropriate box.

'Mussolini's consolidation of power in the period 1922–23 was mainly due to the weaknesses of his opponents.' How far do you agree with this statement?

|  | Support | Challenge |
|---|---|---|
| Parliament granted Mussolini the power to rule by decree. |  |  |
| Mussolini appointed Fascists to key positions in government. |  |  |
| Mussolini appointed liberals and conservatives to key positions in government. |  |  |
| Mussolini gained control of the Fascist movement. |  |  |
| Mussolini established a personal bodyguard to intimidate his opponents. |  |  |
| Parliament passed the Acerbo Law. |  |  |

 **Complete the paragraph**

Below are a sample exam-style question and a paragraph written in answer to this question. The paragraph contains a point and specific examples, but lacks a concluding explanatory link back to the question. Complete the paragraph by adding this link in the space provided.

How accurate is it to say that the consolidation of Fascist power in Italy in the period 1922–23 was mainly due to key political appointments made by Mussolini?

Mussolini's political appointments played a key role in the consolidation of Fascist power in Italy in the period 1922–23. For example, Mussolini appointed Fascist sympathisers to important positions. Alberto De Stefani became Finance Minister and Emilio De Bono was appointed head of the police. In addition, Mussolini appeased liberals and conservatives by giving them posts in his Cabinet. Indeed, his first Cabinet included the same number of liberals as Fascists.

_____

_____

## The consolidation of power 1924–25

The events of 1924 threatened Mussolini's hold on power. However, under pressure from radical Fascists, Mussolini turned a crisis into a dictatorship.

### The 1924 election

The General Election of April 1924 was conducted under the new electoral system. Consequently, Mussolini was determined to win the largest share of the vote and therefore gain control of Parliament. As a result, there was an increased level of MSVN attacks on the socialists in the North. Hundreds of socialists were injured and one **candidate** was killed. Additionally, there was widespread **vote rigging** in Italy's South. These events, and a sophisticated propaganda campaign (see page 40), meant that the **Fascist Bloc** won the largest share of the vote. Consequently, Mussolini gained two-thirds of the seats in the new Parliament.

### The Matteotti Crisis

Following the election, Mussolini faced a crisis that threatened to end his government. At the end of May 1924, Giacomo Matteotti, a leading Socialist, publicly criticised Fascist violence. This resulted in a Fascist gang kidnapping and murdering him.

Many liberals and conservatives, who had previously supported Fascism, became openly critical of Mussolini. Additionally, Socialist deputies withdrew from Parliament in protest at the murder, an act that became known as the 'Aventine Secession'. The crisis deepened as many liberal deputies withdrew their support from Mussolini's government, and unions threatened a **general strike**.

Mussolini responded slowly. Initially, he believed he would be removed from power. However, he continued to receive the King's support. Mussolini turned the crisis to his advantage. In January 1925 he made a speech in which he took personal responsibility for the murder of Matteotti and argued that the violence was necessary to save Italy from the left. His response strengthened his position in his own party, and won him the support of many conservatives who feared the creation of a Socialist government if Mussolini was forced out of power.

### Dictatorship

After dealing with the Matteotti Crisis in a way that strengthened his position, Mussolini introduced a series of reforms in order to create a Fascist dictatorship. The Fascist-dominated Parliament passed laws that:

- banned opposition political parties
- banned trade unions
- established a political police force (see page 42)
- replaced democratically elected local mayors with unelected Fascist officials
- tightened press censorship.

Constitutional changes also strengthened Mussolini's hold on power. First, Parliament lost its right to sack the Prime Minister. Second, Mussolini was granted the right to rule by decree. Unlike the emergency powers, this right was permanent. These two changes effectively ended the independent power of Parliament and established a **personal dictatorship**. Mussolini's new title emphasised his new position: from December 1925 Mussolini was known as **Il Duce** rather than Prime Minister.

### How far was Italy a dictatorship by 1925?

Clearly, by the end of 1925 Mussolini was Italy's dictator though he did not have unlimited power. The constitutional reforms of 1925 essentially made Mussolini independent of Parliament. Additionally, banning other political parties and trade unions, and establishing a political police force, gave Mussolini more power than any Italian leader since unification. However, Mussolini was still accountable to the King and there were important institutions, such as the Roman Catholic Church, that remained independent of Fascist control and therefore limited his power.

Removing obstacles

Mussolini faced a number of obstacles in his plan to establish a Fascist dictatorship in Italy. Use the information on this page and the previous page to complete the table below, explaining how he removed these obstacles to his power.

| Obstacle | Ways in which Mussolini removed this obstacle |
|---|---|
| Other political parties | |
| Independent trades unions | |
| Regular democratic elections | |
| Civil rights | |
| Conservative and liberal aspirations to 'tame' Fascism | |

 Spectrum of significance

Below are a sample exam-style question and a list of general points which could be used to answer the question. Use your own knowledge and the information on the opposite page to reach a judgement about the importance of these general points to the question posed. Write numbers on the spectrum below to indicate their relative importance. Having done this, write a brief justification of your placement, explaining why some of these factors are more important than others. The resulting diagram could form the basis of an essay plan.

How far do you agree that the consolidation of Fascist power in the years 1922–25 was mainly due to the use of terror and violence?

1. The use of terror and violence
2. Emergency powers
3. Key political appointments
4. Mussolini's control of Fascist organisations
5. Political reform
6. The Matteotti Crisis

Less important ⟷ Very important

# Fascist propaganda

Mussolini and other leading Fascists believed that people were fundamentally **irrational**. Therefore, they argued, that they should be led by powerful images and appeals to emotion rather than rational argument. Consequently, the PNF made extensive use of propaganda.

## Propaganda and the consolidation of power

Propaganda played an important role in the consolidation of power. Early Fascist propaganda was relatively sophisticated. For example, during the 1924 election, the PNF targeted different messages at different groups. In middle-class areas, the PNF stressed anti-communism. However, in working-class areas, the radical **Fascist left** produced anti-capitalist propaganda. Older voters were targeted with the message that Fascism had grown out of Italy's ancient culture, whereas younger voters were swayed by hearing how Fascism was a dynamic new force for change.

## The Cult of the Duce

The Cult of the Duce was an important aspect of Fascist propaganda. Mussolini was regularly depicted in two ways, either as an all-powerful leader, or as a **man of the people**. Fascist propaganda used a variety of techniques to emphasise Mussolini's power:

- photographers used low camera angles to hide the fact that he was short
- he was never photographed wearing glasses
- his head was shaved to hide his receding hairline
- he was often photographed excelling at sport
- he was often photographed topless to show off his muscular chest
- he was photographed in various **Napoleonic** poses
- the government launched a campaign featuring the slogan 'Mussolini is always right'.

Photographs of Mussolini laughing with peasants were used to show that Mussolini cared for ordinary people. Additionally, Mussolini's gift for public speaking persuaded many that he shared their concerns.

The Cult of the Duce caused many Italians to believe that Mussolini was the saviour of the nation and therefore above politics. Consequently, the Cult of the Duce strengthened the regime because it persuaded many people who were not Fascists to admire Mussolini.

## The Cult of Rome

Many of Fascism's core values were expressed through the Cult of Rome. Essentially, this aspect of Fascist propaganda linked Mussolini's rule with the greatness of the Roman Empire, which appealed to Italian nationalism. At the same time, it helped justify parts of Fascist rule. For example, Fascist militarism was linked to the Roman army, and Mussolini's dictatorship was compared to the rule of the great Roman Emperors.

## Fascist modernism

The PNF made extensive use of architecture to demonstrate Fascist strength and dynamism. Mussolini's regime was the greatest patron of **modernist** architecture in the world during the interwar period. The Esposizione Universale Roma (EUR) was the largest building project during Mussolini's reign. The EUR was an extension of Rome designed to combine housing apartments, monuments and government buildings. Construction started in 1935. Though parts of it, such as the **Palazzo della Civiltà Italiana**, were completed, the rest was not built due to the Second World War. Major projects included the **Foro Mussolini** and the **Piazza augusto imperatore**. Fascist architecture helped promote the regime through futuristic design, creating an image of a new Fascist **utopia** as great as the ancient Roman Empire.

## Eliminate irrelevance

Below are a sample exam-style question and a paragraph written in answer to this question. Read the paragraph and identify parts of the paragraph that are not directly relevant to the question. Draw a line through the information that is irrelevant and justify your deletions in the margin.

How far do you agree that the consolidation of Fascist power in Italy in the years 1922–25 was mainly due to the use of propaganda?

One way in which propaganda was used to consolidate Fascist power in Italy in the years 1922–25 was through the Cult of the Duce. This involved using propaganda to depict Mussolini as the saviour of Italy. For example, Mussolini was often portrayed as an all-powerful leader. He was photographed in Napoleonic poses to suggest similarities between himself and the French leader. Both Mussolini and Napoleon were said to be short. However, it is now thought that Napoleon was of average height. The government also launched a campaign with the slogan 'Mussolini is always right'. In addition, Mussolini was pictured with peasants to suggest that he was a man of the people and that he was in touch with their concerns. Furthermore, Mussolini censored the press to ensure that anti-Fascist articles were not published. In this way, the Cult of the Duce played an important role in the consolidation of Fascist power in Italy in the period 1922–25 because it persuaded many people that Mussolini's leadership was good for Italy.

## Develop the detail

Below are a sample exam-style question and a paragraph written in answer to this question. The paragraph contains a limited amount of detail. Annotate the paragraph to add additional detail to the answer.

How far do you agree that Fascist control of Italy in the years 1922–43 was mainly the result of the use of propaganda?

Propaganda played an important role in establishing and maintaining Fascist control over Italy in the period 1922–43. Early Fascist propaganda targeted different social groups with different messages. In addition, the Cult of the Duce was used to suggest that Mussolini was a strong leader. The Cult of Rome was used to suggest that there were clear links between Fascist Italy and the Roman Empire. Finally, modernist architecture was used to suggest that the regime was creating a new Fascist utopia. In this way, propaganda was used to establish and maintain Fascist control of Italy in the period 1922–43 by encouraging people to see the regime as strong and dynamic, and drawing parallels between the Fascist regime and Ancient Rome.

## Fascist terror

Terror was a central part of the Fascist consolidation of power. Following 1926, Fascist use of terror was less obvious but no less important in sustaining Mussolini's government.

### Terror and the consolidation of power

From 1922 to 1926, Mussolini used terror to strengthen his hold on power. For example:

- The *squadristi* threatened revolutionary violence immediately prior to the March on Rome.
- The *squadristi* terrorised socialists and union members.
- Approximately 2000 political opponents were murdered between 1922 and 1925.
- The MSVN intimidated voters during the 1924 election.

### The OVRA

The **OVRA**, Mussolini's political police, were established in November 1926. Originally, they were tasked with combating anti-Fascist groups. However, over time their role grew and they came to keep large sections of society under surveillance.

### The scale of OVRA activity

The OVRA were much smaller than the political police in **Stalin's Russia** or **Hitler's Germany** during the 1930s. The OVRA only had 700 agents, and the political prison camps established on islands, such as Lipari and Lampedusa never held more than 6000 political prisoners. Yet, by 1930 they had created a network of 100,000 informants. Bar owners were often required to work as police informants to gain business permits. Additionally, doctors were legally required to report a variety of medical conditions that the PNF believed indicated political problems, including mental illness, alcoholism and **venereal disease**. By 1943, the OVRA had files on 130,000 citizens and conducted an average of 20,000 raids every week. Consequently, though OVRA membership was small, its large network of informants and regular raids created a widespread

atmosphere of terror which helped discourage anti-Fascist activity.

### Fascist justice

The persecution of political opponents was formalised through the creation of the Special Tribunal for the Defence of the State. Between 1927 and 1943 the Special Tribunal:

- found 4596 people guilty of political crimes
- passed sentences totalling 27,735 years of imprisonment.

In addition, the Tribunal passed 42 death sentences. Significantly, only nine death sentences were passed during peacetime and of the 42 sentences passed, only 31 were carried out.

### Fascist anti-Semitism

At the end of the 1930s, the Fascist government began to persecute Italy's Jewish minority. Mussolini's introduction of **anti-Semitic** laws reflected his increasing respect for Hitler's Nazi regime in Germany. Mussolini's racist decrees, issued between November 1938 and June 1939, did the following:

- banned marriage between Jews and non-Jews
- banned Jews from serving in the armed forces
- banned Jews from owning large areas of land
- expelled Jewish teachers and students from schools and universities
- expelled Jews from the civil service
- banned foreign Jews from entering Italy.

By the late 1930s, 7000 Jews had been forced to leave the armed forces, and 5600 Jewish students and 181 Jewish teachers were forced out of schools and universities.

Finally, when Italy entered the Second World War in 1940, all non-Italian Jews living in Italy were sent to prison camps. During 1941 the Italian government tried to expel non-Italian Jews from Italy, and, a year later, Mussolini agreed to send all Jews in Italy to Nazi **extermination camps**. Evidently, anti-Semitism became increasingly important to Fascist policy as the regime developed.

Turning assertion into argument

Below are a sample exam-style question and two assertions. Read the exam-style question and then add a justification to each of the assertions to turn it into an argument.

How far do you agree that fascist control of Italy in the years 1922–43 was mainly the result of terror?

Terror played an essential role in Mussolini's consolidation of power in the sense that

_____

_____

The OVRA played a key role in maintaining Fascist control of Italy in the sense that

_____

_____

 You're the examiner

Below are a sample exam-style question and a paragraph written in answer to this question. Read the paragraph and the mark scheme provided on page 3. Decide which level you would award the paragraph. Write the level below, along with a justification for your choice.

How far do you agree that Fascist control of Italy in the years 1922–43 was mainly the result of terror?

Mussolini established the OVRA, his political police, in 1926 and they helped to maintain Fascist control over Italy. They had only 700 agents, but by 1930 had established a network of 100,000 informants. People in certain professions, such as doctors and bar owners, were required to provide information to the OVRA. For example, doctors were required to report on patients with alcoholism and mental illness. By 1943, the OVRA held files on 143,000 citizens and conducted about 20,000 raids every week. However, the prison camps for political prisoners never held more than 6000 inmates.

Level:          Reason for choosing this level:

_____

_____

## Women and children

### Young people

Fascists aimed to inspire a new generation. They wanted to turn young people into **homo fascistus**, a new type of human that would serve the nation selflessly.

### The Battle for Births

The 'Battle for Births' policy was introduced in 1927. It was designed to increase the number of children being born. Consequently, the policy impacted on women and family life.

Prior to the March on Rome there was considerable public debate concerning the birth rate. There were concerns that the millions of deaths in the First World War would lead to **depopulation**, and that Italy risked being conquered by Russia, which had a much higher population. Therefore, in 1927 Mussolini introduced measures to increase the Italian population from 40 to 60 million by 1950:

- Contraception and abortion were banned.
- Unmarried men paid higher tax rates than married men.
- Married men with six or more children paid no tax.
- A family allowance was introduced to help support families.
- A marriage loan was introduced, and partly paid off by the government after the birth of a child.
- A propaganda campaign ridiculed **flappers**, feminists and women who did not prioritise motherhood.

Other policies designed to encourage more births included:

- the banning of homosexuality in 1931
- the number of places for young women in secondary school was reduced
- the total number of women working in the Civil Service was reduced to 10 per cent in 1933
- a 10 per cent cap on women workers was introduced into most industries in 1938.

### Impact on births

Overall, the policy was a failure. Marriage rates stagnated, and the birth rate declined from 1927 to 1936. There was a small increase from 1936, but even in the late 1930s the birth rate of 102 births per 1000 was lower than the 1911 birth rate of 147 per 1000.

### Impact on women

Mussolini failed to exclude women from the work force. This was partly due to the fact that Fascist laws reflected traditional gender stereotypes. Therefore, the PNF did not try to exclude women from occupations such as waitressing and typing. Additionally, the PNF were willing to allow women to work as teachers. Therefore, by 1936, 75 per cent of trainee teachers were women. Nonetheless, even when the PNF actively tried to exclude women they failed. For example, by 1938 women made up 28 per cent of the industrial labour force and 38 per cent of agricultural workers.

Finally, the Fascist campaign against flappers and feminists failed. In urban areas, women, who became known as '*la maschietta*', continued to wear an **androgynous** fashion style throughout the 1930s.

### Fascist militarism

Militarism was an important part of Fascist ideology. Essentially, Fascists believed that the military was the best form of organisation, as it inspired courage, discipline and self-sacrifice. They argued that all institutions, including the government, the family, businesses and schools, should be organised like the army.

Fascist militarism was reflected in Mussolini's use of the word 'battle' to describe key policies. It was a growing feature of Fascist government in the 1930s. For example, in 1932 the handshake was replaced by a military salute as the official greeting within the civil service. Additionally, civil servants were expected to stand to attention when speaking to their superiors on the telephone.

## Spider diagram

Use the information on the opposite page to add detail to the spider diagram below.

Evidence of success — **The Battle for Births** — Evidence of failure

## Delete as applicable

Below are a sample exam-style question and a paragraph written in answer to this question. Read the paragraph and decide which of the possible options (underlined) is most appropriate. Delete the least appropriate options and complete the paragraph by justifying your selection.

How far do you agree that Mussolini's social policies were successful?

Mussolini's Battle for Births was successful to a <u>great/fair/limited</u> extent. For example, the birth rate declined in the period 1927 to 1936, and despite an increase in the birth rate from 1936, the 1911 birth rate of 147 per 1000 was never exceeded. Furthermore, the Battle for Births failed to reduce the number of women in the workforce. By 1938, 28 per cent of the industrial labour force and 38 per cent of agricultural labourers were women. In addition, by 1936, 75 per cent of those training to be teachers were women. In this way, Mussolini's Battle for Births was <u>extremely/moderately/slightly</u> successful because

_____

_____

## Education and censorship

The PNF used education to instil 'correct' Fascist values, and censorship to eliminate anti-Fascist values from the media.

### Schools and universities

Mussolini took several steps to control education:

- In 1925, he ordered a **purge**, removing teachers and lecturers who did not support Fascism.
- He tightened control in 1929, when teachers and lecturers were forced to swear an oath to the King and to Fascism.
- In 1933 teachers and lecturers were required to join the PNF.
- In 1934 teachers and lecturers were required to wear the black shirt uniform.

### The curriculum

The Ministry of Education revised the curriculum to reflect Fascist values. Consequently, a third of all history textbooks were banned in 1926. From 1937, all secondary school children were required to take an exam on the achievements of Fascism. Universities were required to offer a new course on the history and **doctrine** of Fascism.

A new School Charter was introduced in 1939 to link schools and the PNF more closely. However, the Charter was never fully implemented due to the Second World War.

### Youth groups

The regime also tried to influence young people outside of school. In 1926, the Ministry established the *Opera Nazionale Balilla* (ONB) as a Fascist youth movement. The ONB attracted millions of members due to their sports clubs and summer camps. The PNF took control of it in 1937 and renamed it *Gioventu Italiana del Littorio* (GIL). The ONB became compulsory in 1939, by which point it had almost 8 million members. University students were encouraged to join the *Gioventu Universitaria Fascista* (GUL). GUL organised social activities but **ostracised** female students.

### Censorship

In the early years of the regime, the PNF focused on **censorship**. However, after the creation of the Ministry of Popular Culture (Minculpop), they began to use the media to **indoctrinate** the public.

### The press

Press censorship was one of Mussolini's priorities immediately following the March on Rome. He began by removing the anti-Fascist editors of popular papers such as *La Stampa* and *Corriere della Sera*.

Mussolini introduced tougher censorship laws in response to press outrage at Matteotti's murder. Initially Mussolini claimed that these were temporary. However, by the end of 1925 he decreed that all newspaper editors had to be members of the Association of Fascist Journalists. By the end of 1926, opposition newspapers had been closed, and in early 1927 the establishment of new papers was banned. Initially, the Press and Information Office organised press censorship, but in 1929 the PNF established the High Commission to do this.

### Cinema

From 1924 the Censorship Board censored all films. The Board comprised a judge, a mother (who represented ordinary Italians), and an official from the **Office of Public Security**. In the same year, the regime founded the *Istituto Luce* which was responsible for making public information films. These pro-government films were shown in cinemas before feature films.

### Minculpop

Fascist policy changed radically in 1937. Existing Fascist censorship was abolished and replaced with the Minculpop. The new ministry focused more on projecting a positive image of the regime than censorship. Minculpop issued detailed orders to the press, and vigorously promoted the anti-Semitic campaign of the late 1930s (see page 42). Minculpop encouraged film makers to glorify obedience and portray women as submissive.

## Spectrum of success

Below is a sample exam-style question and a list of general points which could be used to answer the question. Use your own knowledge and the information on the opposite page to reach a judgement about the success of the policies relating to each point. Write numbers on the spectrum below to indicate their relative success. Having done this, write a brief justification of your placement, explaining why some of these policies are more successful than others. The resulting diagram could form the basis of an essay plan.

How far do you agree that Mussolini's social policies were successful?

1. The Battle for Births
2. Education
3. Youth groups

Less successful ← ──────────────────────────────── → Very successful

## Introducing an argument

Below are a sample exam-style question, a list of key points to be made in the essay, and a simple introduction and conclusion for the essay. Read the question, the plan, and the introduction and conclusion. Rewrite the introduction and the conclusion to develop an argument.

How far did Mussolini transform the lives of women and children in the period 1922–43?

**Key points:**

- Women – home life
- Women – work
- Children – education
- Children – youth groups

**Introduction**

> Mussolini transformed the lives of women and children to an extent. He changed the lives of women in terms of home life and work. In addition, he changed the lives of children in terms of education and youth groups.

**Conclusion**

> Overall, Mussolini transformed the lives of women and children to an extent. He changed the expectations regarding women's home life and working life. He also changed children's school and leisure time.

## Fascist economic policy

Revised

Between 1922 and 1943, Mussolini adopted a series of different economic policies.

### Liberal economics 1922–26

Mussolini's initial economic policy addressed Italy's massive budget deficit. To tackle this, the Minister of Finance, De Stefani:

- made large cuts in **public spending**
- **privatised** government owned companies, including Italy's telephone company, the government pension services, and the railways
- introduced **deregulation**
- reduced taxation to encourage business growth.

In the short term De Stefani's policies were successful. Government debt shrank from 74.8 per cent of GDP in 1922 to 50.6 per cent of GDP in 1925. At the same time, industrial production increased by 57 per cent between 1922 and 1925. However, the economic recovery, and a poor grain harvest in 1924, created rising inflation and a **balance of payments** deficit. Consequently, the value of Italian currency fell from 91.5 lira to the pound in 1922 to 144.9 lira to the pound in 1925.

Mussolini responded by replacing De Stefani with Giuseppe Volpi, a decision which led to a radical change in economic policy.

### The foundations of Corporatism 1926–29

Volpi replaced De Stefani's **laissez-faire economics** with Corporatism, establishing the Ministry of Corporations in 1926. In theory, Corporatism brought representatives of the state, workers and management together to serve the interests of the nation. In practice, Corporatism was used to extend state control over the economy. Government intervention was also reflected in other initiatives such the Battle for Grain.

### Battle for Grain

The 'Battle for Grain' was designed to mobilise Italians to boost grain production. This, in turn, would lead to a reduction in grain imports, which accounted for 50 per cent of Italy's imports in 1925, and therefore a healthier balance of payments.

The campaign successfully increased grain production from an annual average of 5.5 million tonnes in the early 1920s to around 7 million tonnes in the early 1930s. Consequently, grain imports dropped by 75 per cent. However, Italy lost a significant source of income as many farmers stopped producing citrus fruits so they could produce grain.

Following the 'Battle for Grain', Mussolini began the 'Battle for the Lira': a policy of revaluing the lira at 90 to the pound. Mussolini argued that the higher value reflected Italy's new greatness, however it also made Italy's exports uncompetitive.

### Corporatism 1929–43

During the 1930s, Corporatism grew in several ways:

- The National Council of Corporations was established in 1930 to advise the government on economic policy.
- Twenty-two national corporations were established in 1934, representing workers, business and the state. These helped regulate industry and played a role in labour relations.

### Autarky 1935–43

Autarky was a policy designed to make Italy economically self-sufficient. Mussolini adopted the policy to protect Italy from the effect of economic sanctions imposed by the **League of Nations** following Italy's invasion of Abyssinia (see page 60).

The implementation of autarky had some success. For example, aluminium production increased, and new synthetic materials, such as lanital, were developed to replace imported natural fibres. However, Italy was able to produce only a quarter of the country's oil needs, and only 1.8 million tonnes of iron ore annually, less than a tenth of production in Germany. Generally, autarky failed, as domestic production could generate only a fifth of the goods that Italy needed.

## Spider diagram

Use the information on the opposite page to add detail to the spider diagram below.

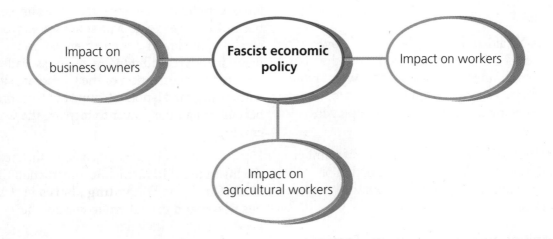

Impact on business owners — Fascist economic policy — Impact on workers — Impact on agricultural workers

## Develop the detail

Below are a sample exam-style question and a paragraph written in answer to this question. The paragraph contains a limited amount of detail. Annotate the paragraph to add additional detail to the answer.

How successful were Mussolini's economic policies in the period 1922–43?

The Battle for Grain is an example of an economic policy that was largely successful. The campaign was designed to increase grain production in Italy. The campaign was successful at increasing grain production. This led to a significant drop in grain imports. However, the campaign was not entirely successful. Many farmers stopped producing citrus fruits to produce grain instead. This had an impact on the economy. In this way, the Battle for Grain was very successful at meeting its aim of increasing grain production, but it had a mixed effect on Italy's balance of payments situation.

## Fascism and the traditional elites

Fascists saw themselves as a new elite who would replace the old elites that had failed to ensure that Italy gained what it deserved after the war. However, in practice they were often forced to work with powerful traditional elites.

### The Church

Rather than challenging the power of the Roman Catholic Church, the Fascist regime sought compromise and collaboration.

**Pope Pius XI** aided the consolidation of power, arguing that the Church should work with the PNF to combat communism. Mussolini also won favour with Pius XI by using government money to save the Catholic Bank of Rome from bankruptcy in 1923.

Between 1926 and 1943, Mussolini took a number of steps to win the support of the Church. For example, he banned abortion and outlawed the sale of contraceptives in 1926.

### The significance of the Lateran Treaties

The Lateran Treaties of 1929 created a closer relationship between the Fascist regime and the Church by resolving long-standing problems. The Treaties agreed:

- The independence of the Vatican.
- An amount of financial compensation for the Vatican's losses of territory during Italian unification.
- A **Concordat**: the Church would support the government, Roman Catholicism would become Italy's official religion, and the government would respect the Church's rights to play a role in education.

The Treaties ended the division between the Church and the state, and guaranteed the Church's support for the regime.

However, the Treaties did not resolve every problem. For example, the PNF were suspicious that anti-Fascist campaigners were using **Catholic Action** to organise themselves against the regime. Additionally, in the late 1930s, the Pope was critical of the anti-Semitic aspects of the regime.

### Business elites

The regime's relationship with business elites changed over time. Mussolini played down the corporatist aspects of Fascism between 1922 and 1925 to appease Italian business, which was opposed to state interference. Equally, businesses supported Mussolini's abolition of independent trade unions.

However, there were tensions. For example, export businesses objected to Mussolini's policy of revaluing the lira as it made their exports uncompetitive. Additionally, business leaders objected to the creation of the Corporate state, particularly the National Council of Corporations, because it had the power to increase the wages of employees.

Finally, business leaders objected to the creation of the Institute for Industrial Reconstruction (IIR) in 1933. The IIR bought **voting shares** in private businesses and used them to control the development of Italian industry.

### Agricultural elites

From 1922, the PNF tended to compromise with the agricultural elites because it needed their support in rural areas. Initially, radical Fascists wanted to liberate the peasants by eliminating the old agricultural elites. However, following the March on Rome, Mussolini sidelined rural radicals to retain the support of the powerful agricultural elite. For example, in 1923 Mussolini expelled the leading Fascist radical in Naples, Aurelio Padovani, from the PNF for demanding a social revolution in the countryside. Agricultural elites grew rich, gaining large government subsidies for administering policies such as the Battle for Grain (see page 48). Additionally, powerful figures in the PNF, such as Italo Balbo, fought consistently for the interests of the agricultural elites of his home province of Ferrara. Balbo, like Mussolini, recognised that the PNF could not govern the countryside without the support of the agricultural elites.

## RAG – Rate the timeline

Below are a sample exam-style question and a timeline. Read the question, study the timeline and, using three coloured pens, put a red, amber or green star next to the events to show:

- red – events and policies that have no relevance to the question
- amber – events and policies that have some significance to the question
- green – events and policies that are directly relevant to the question.

1) How far do you agree that the Catholic Church and the traditional elites were the main beneficiaries of Fascist government in the period 1922–43?

Now repeat the activity with the following questions:

2) How far do you agree that it was Mussolini's use of conciliation, rather than his use of terror, that enabled him to consolidate his power in the period 1922–29?

3) How far do you agree that Mussolini's social and economic policies were successful in the period 1922–43?

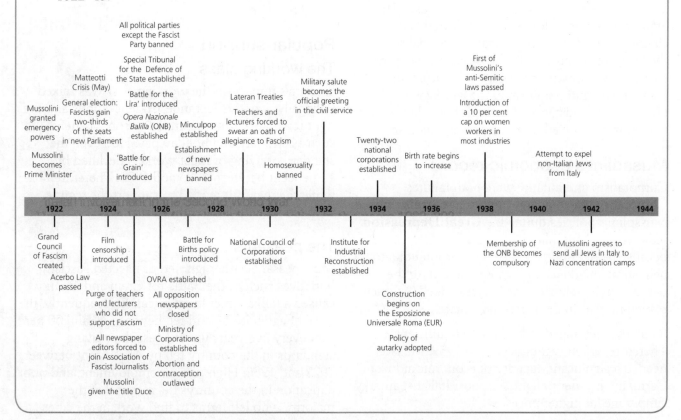

## Simple essay style

Now use your own knowledge and the information on the opposite page to produce a plan for each of the questions above. Choose four general points, and provide three pieces of specific information to support each general point. Once you have planned your essay, write the introduction and conclusion for the essay. The introduction should list the points to be discussed in the essay. The conclusion should summarise the key points and justify which point was the most important.

# How successful was Fascism 1922–43?

Mussolini aimed to create a **totalitarian state**, a dynamic dictatorship in which all citizens were totally committed to their leader. In reality, Fascist Italy failed to live up to Mussolini's vision.

## Mussolini's dictatorship

Mussolini took several steps to strengthen his hold on power after 1925. First, he reformed the PNF to ensure it was under his personal control. A year later, the Grand Council approved a new **party statute** that replaced election from below with appointment from above. This strengthened Mussolini's position by giving him the power of **patronage**. Second, in 1931 he appointed Achille Starace as Party Secretary, replacing Augusto Turati. Starace was wholly loyal, whereas Turati had clashed with Mussolini and was a potential rival for the leadership of the PNF. The Lateran Treaties also ensured the support of the Church, at least until conflict over anti-Semitism in the late 1930s. However, the existence of powerful old elites shows that Mussolini failed to create a totalitarian state.

## Mussolini's economic record

Corporatism and autarky were both failures. Corporatism created large inefficient **cartels**. Indeed, Mussolini's policies during the **Great Depression** indicate that Mussolini had no faith in Corporatism, because he did not try to use the Corporations to help stimulate the economy. Rather, during the depression he relied on the IIR (see page 50) which played no part in the Corporatist State.

Similarly, Italy failed to become self-sufficient. Therefore, when war broke out in 1939, Mussolini needed a significant quantity of economic aid from Germany in order to fight. For most Italians, autarky simply meant higher prices.

However, unemployment remained relatively low. During the Great Depression the regime introduced **public works** schemes such as **land reclamation** in the Pontine Marshes to create jobs. Therefore, Italy's use of **Keynesian policies** meant that unemployment in Italy in the early 1930s was around 15 per cent, lower than the 22 per cent in Britain and 30 per cent in Germany during the same period. Additionally, government arms spending rose from 7 million lira in 1935 to 14 million lira in 1936, creating new jobs in arms production.

Despite this, Fascism failed to help Italy catch up with other European economies. Between 1922 and 1938 Italy averaged an annual 1.9 per cent growth in GDP, whereas the average across western Europe was 2.5 per cent.

## Popular support
### The working class

Fascism's impact on the working class was mixed. Politically, workers lost independent unions and the right to strike. Corporatism led to some benefits such as sick pay and holiday pay. However, the standard of living of most workers declined by 11 per cent between 1925 and 1938. Therefore, while the majority tended to support the regime, they did so with little enthusiasm.

### The peasants

Most peasants either ignored or rejected Fascism. Initiatives such as the Battle for Grain and autarky caused a fall in agricultural prices. Consequently, the price of agricultural land fell between 40 and 50 per cent every five years under Mussolini. Living standards in the country fell by 40 per cent between 1922 and 1930. High rural unemployment, and poor education in the countryside, meant that the majority who left farms to find work in the cities were unsuccessful.

## Support or challenge?

Below is a sample exam-style question which asks how far you agree with a specific statement. Below this are a series of general statements which are relevant to the question. Using your own knowledge and the information on the opposite page decide whether these statements support or challenge the statement in the question and tick the appropriate box.

'Mussolini was successful in creating a totalitarian state in Italy in the period 1922–43'. How far do you agree with this statement?

| | Support | Challenge |
|---|---|---|
| The Lateran Treaties brought about a closer relationship between the Catholic Church and the Fascist regime. | | |
| Many workers supported the regime, though with little enthusiasm. | | |
| Many peasants did not support Fascism. | | |
| By 1930, the OVRA had a network of 100,000 informants. | | |
| Between 1927 and 1943, the Special Tribunal found 4596 people guilty of political crimes. | | |
| By 1938, women made up 38 per cent of the industrial labour force. | | |
| Fascist propaganda encouraged people to see the regime as strong and dynamic. | | |
| Mussolini's social policies aimed to control aspects of people's private lives. | | |
| Membership of the ONB was made compulsory in 1939. | | |
| Corporatism was used to extend state control over the economy. | | |

## Recommended reading

Below is a list of suggested further reading on this topic.

- *Italy: The Rise of Fascism 1915–1945*, chapters 4 to 7, Mark Robson (2006)
- *Modern Italy, 1871 to the Present*, pages 266–334, Martin Clark (2008)
- *Mussolini and Italy*, pages 41–96 and 159–196, Edward Townley (2002)

## Exam focus

Below is a sample A grade essay. Read it and the examiner comments around it.

How successful were Fascism's political and economic policies in the years 1922 to 1940?

The introduction sets out a range of factors to be discussed. Significantly, it considers both aspects of the question as it deals with the successes of political and economic policies.

Fascism was largely successful in terms of politics between the years 1922 and 1940 because Mussolini was able to consolidate power and win the support of Italy's major elites. However, Mussolini was never able to fully transform Italy's politics as his attempts to create a totalitarian state and a new 'fascist man' failed. Fascist economic policies were much less successful, as the Italian economy performed less well under Mussolini than it had during the 'Giolitti period' and less well than other major economies in the interwar years.

This paragraph contains a great deal of detail, including precise statistics, about the various policies used to consolidate power.

Fascism's political and economic policies led to the successful consolidation of power in the years 1922 to 1925. For example, Mussolini demanded and received the emergency power to rule by decree, making him independent of the Italian Parliament. Mussolini was also able to impose control over his own movement by disciplining the squadristi by turning it into a state-funded Fascist Militia, the MSVN. Additionally, the creation of the Grand Council of Fascism in 1922 allowed Mussolini to dominate the leadership of the Fascist movement. These measures allowed Mussolini to claim that he had 'tamed' the Fascist movement and won him support from conservatives and liberals in Parliament. Consequently, in November 1923, Mussolini was able to pass the Giacomo Acerbo's Electoral Law which led to a PNF-dominated Parliament following the 1924 election. Fascist economic policy was also initially successful as it reduced government debt from 74.8 per cent of GDP in 1922 to 50.6 per cent of GDP in 1925. Finally, following the Matteotti Crisis, Mussolini was able to establish a dictatorship through a series of constitutional reforms which banned opposition political parties and independent trades unions, established a political police (the OVRA) and gave Mussolini the power to rule by decree permanently. In this way, Fascism's political and economic policies were clearly successful in the period 1922 to 1925 as they allowed Mussolini to consolidate power by creating a Fascist dictatorship.

Here, the essay demonstrates a range of knowledge by considering three different elite groups.

Fascism's political polices were also successful as they allowed the government to win the support of important elite groups. For example, the Lateran Treaties of 1929 established a close relationship between the Roman Catholic Church and the PNF government. In return for an independent state, financial compensation and the promise that the PNF would respect the rights of the Church, the Pope promised to support the Fascist regime. Business leaders and the middle class were won over by Mussolini's anti-communism and his anti-union policies. Finally, the agricultural elite was won over by the taming of radical aspects of Fascism that focused on peasant rights. Specifically, by the end of 1923 Mussolini had expelled or sidelined Fascist radicals like Aurelio Padovani who wanted a social revolution in the countryside. In this way, Fascism's political policies were successful because they secured the regime by ensuring the support of the major elites.

The analysis of connections between the success of winning over the elites and the failure to create a genuinely totalitarian state effectively links different aspects of the essay creating sustained analysis.

However, Fascism's political polices were not wholly successful as they failed to create a totalitarian state or a fascist 'new man.' Mussolini's key political aim was to create a totalitarian state, a state with total control over society where all citizens were committed to Fascist values. However, Mussolini failed to do this. Mussolini's success in winning over the elites is evidence that he failed to create a totalitarian regime, as a truly totalitarian regime would have completely dominated the whole of society rather than having to compromise with non-Fascist groups. The continued power of the Church, the King, business and land owners shows that totalitarianism was never achieved. Also, the PNF never created homo fascistus, a new 'fascist man' who was selflessly and totally committed to Fascist values. This is clear from the failure of policies such as the Battle for Births. In spite of propaganda and incentives birth rates remained lower than they had been in 1911 and marriage rates stagnated, indicating a lack of commitment to this key Fascist goal. Clearly, Fascism's political polices failed in these key areas as old elites were never fully dominated and Italian citizens continued to live according to non-Fascist values.

Overall, Fascist economic policies were a failure. The initial success in reducing government debt under Minister of Finance, De Stefani, led to new problems such as the a balance of payments deficit and a drop in the value of the lira. Equally, although the Italian economy grew, growth rates were not impressive. Between 1922 and 1938, Italian GDP grew by an average of 1.9 per cent. However, this was less impressive than growth during the 'Giolitti period' in which the GDP grew at an annual average of 2.8 per cent. Additionally, Italy's growth of 1.9 per cent a year under Mussolini was worse than average across western Europe which was 2.5 per cent in the interwar years. Specific policies also failed. Autarky, for example, only produced a fifth of the products that Italy needed. Finally, the standard of living of the working class declined by 11 per cent between 1925 and 1938. Again, this is worse than the 'Giolitti period' in which the standard of living grew by an average of 2.1 per cent a year. Clearly, Fascist economic policies were a failure because growth rates were poor compared to other periods in Italian history and compared to other European countries during the same period and because Mussolini's key policies such as autarky failed to achieve their aims.

Overall, Fascism's political and economic policies in the years 1922 to 1940 were only moderately successful. Fascism's biggest success was the consolidation of power that took place between 1922 and 1925, ending the establishment of a Fascist dictatorship. However, successful compromise with other elites undermined the success of creating a totalitarian regime or a new 'fascist man', as the compromise with other elites ensured that there were other powerful institutions in society and therefore that other values, particularly Roman Catholic values, continued to compete with Fascist values. Fascist economic policies failed in general terms and specific terms, as growth was relatively poor and policies such as autarky never achieved their goals.

This paragraph effectively analyses the failure of Fascist economic policies by comparing precise statistics from another period and other countries.

The conclusion summarises the argument of the essay reaching an overall judgement about the success of Fascist policy. Significantly it addresses both economic and political aspects of the question, and emphasises the link that the essay made between the successes of some aspects of policy and the failure of others.

28/30

This gets into Level 5 because of the sustained focus on evaluating the success of political and economic policies and the way the essay links successes in some areas with failures in others. The focus and detail are excellent throughout. More links between the factors or an overall argument would have gained the essay maximum marks.

## Reverse engineering

The best essays are based on careful plans. Read the essay, and the examiner's comments, and try to work out the general points of the plan used to write the essay. Once you have done this, note down the specific examples used to support each general point.

# Section 4:
# Building the new Roman Empire

## Mussolini's foreign policy aims

Mussolini's ultimate foreign policy aim was to make Italy a great nation. This reflected his Fascist ideology as well as his desire to gain what Italy had failed to achieve in the 'mutilated victory' (see page 18). Essentially, Mussolini wanted to create a new Roman Empire, including **colonies** in the Balkans, around the Mediterranean, and in Africa.

### Ideology and foreign policy

War and empire were important parts of Fascist ideology. Unlike most liberals and socialists, Fascists believed that warfare was an essential part of life because:

■ Warfare brought out the best in nations and individuals. War led to national unity and turned soldiers into 'real men' by teaching them heroism and self-sacrifice.

■ Building an empire and conquering other countries were key to national greatness. Fascists believed that Britain and France had become great through establishing empires in Africa, Asia and the Caribbean, and argued that Italy could only do this by creating overseas colonies which would provide the **motherland** with vital resources.

■ As **social Darwinists**, Fascists believed that warfare was natural and led to the survival of the fittest nations. Specifically, Mussolini believed Britain and France were **decadent** nations who had become weak and therefore no longer had the right to dominate the world. Italy, by contrast, was an up-and-coming, dynamic nation that deserved to replace the old empires as a major global power.

### Territorial goals

Mussolini had a series of territorial goals. He wanted to:

■ consolidate Italy's hold on its existing Empire in Italian North Africa (now Libya) and Italian East Africa (now Somalia)

■ gain territory in Abyssinia (now Ethiopia)

■ gain control of the Balkan ports around the Adriatic Sea, including Fiume and Corfu. Mussolini viewed control of the Adriatic as the first step to naval dominance of the Mediterranean Sea.

■ break British and French control over the Mediterranean Sea and establish the Mediterranean Sea as 'Italy's lake'.

### Fascist foreign policy

In spite of Mussolini's ideology, Fascist foreign policy was not initially warlike. Fascist foreign policy changed over time. Nonetheless, Mussolini made the major foreign policy decisions throughout the whole period.

From 1922 to 1935 Mussolini largely avoided conflict with other major nations. He gained the respect of Britain and France who viewed him as a strong, pragmatic **statesman**. However, in the mid-1930s his policy became more aggressive. As a result, Mussolini formed closer links with Hitler's Germany.

Use the information on the opposite page to add detail to the spider diagram below.

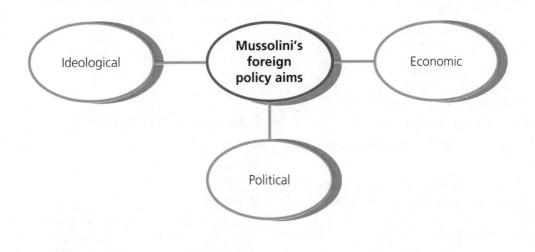

Below is a sample exam-style question which asks how far you agree with a specific statement. Below this are a series of general statements which are relevant to the question. Using your own knowledge and the information on the opposite page, decide whether these statements support or challenge the statement in the question and tick the appropriate box.

'In the years 1922–43, Mussolini's foreign policy aims were wholly ideological.' How far do you agree with this statement?

| | Support | Challenge |
|---|---|---|
| Mussolini wanted to make Italy a great nation. | | |
| Mussolini hoped that the success of his foreign policy would compensate for the 'mutilated victory' following the First World War. | | |
| Mussolini believed that war led to national unity. | | |
| Mussolini believed that overseas colonies would provide Italy with important resources. | | |
| Mussolini wanted to establish Italian dominance of the Mediterranean Sea. | | |
| Before 1935, Mussolini avoided conflict with other major nations. | | |
| Mussolini believed that Britain and France were becoming weak and that it was Italy's turn to become a global power. | | |

## Fiume and Corfu

### Foreign policy 1922–29

During Mussolini's period as Foreign Secretary, from 1922 to 1929, there was little change in Italian foreign policy. Mussolini adopted a cautious approach for several reasons:

- From 1922 to 1924, nationalists and liberals still dominated the Foreign Office.
- Foreign policy experts **Raffaele Guariglia** and Dino Grandi persuaded Mussolini to continue Italy's traditional policy of moderation.
- Italy could not afford to go to war.
- Mussolini was keen to gain the respect of Britain and France.

Nonetheless, Mussolini made two attempts to gain overseas territory in the years 1922 to 1929.

### The Corfu incident

Mussolini wanted control of Corfu because the Greek island's position in the Adriatic Sea was crucial for dominance over the Mediterranean Sea. Therefore, Mussolini attempted to exploit a crisis to achieve his goal. In 1923 three Italian diplomats, who were working with the League of Nations, were murdered. Mussolini responded by demanding 50 million lire in compensation. When Greece refused, Mussolini ordered the bombardment and occupation of Corfu. International pressure and Greece's eventual agreement to compensate Italy forced the Italian army to withdraw. The Italian press presented this resolution as a victory because Italy had forced Greece to pay. However, Mussolini had failed to retain control of Corfu.

### Fiume

The **Annexation** of Fiume was Mussolini's first major foreign policy success. In March 1923, Mussolini sent Italian troops into Fiume, claiming revolutionaries were threatening the port. This effectively established Italian control over Fiume. Italy's position was confirmed in January 1924 by the Treaty of Rome, an agreement between Italy and Yugoslavia that Fiume should become part of Italy.

The Annexation of Fiume was highly popular, and played a part in the early consolidation of the Fascist regime. It allowed Mussolini to claim that he was standing up for Italy's interests. Additionally, the Italian media presented Mussolini's policy as a heroic adventure similar to D'Annunzio's occupation of Fiume following the First World War (see page 26).

### Foreign policy 1925–29

Mussolini signed two treaties during this period that strengthened Italy's relationship with Britain and France:

- In 1925, Italy signed the Locarno Pact. The Pact consolidated the border between France and Germany. Indeed, if war broke out between France and Germany, the Pact committed Britain and Italy to defend the country that had been attacked.
- In 1928, Mussolini signed the Kellogg–Briand Pact. The treaty committed 54 nations to settle any differences through negotiations rather than war.

### Successes and failures 1922–29

Mussolini did little to create a new Roman Empire. There were clear gains, such as Fiume. Additionally, Britain agreed to hand over territory to both of Italy's African colonies. However, Britain was still the dominant power in the Mediterranean and Africa. Moreover, Mussolini had gained nothing from the Locarno Pact. While the Pact guaranteed the French border it did nothing to stop Germany expanding in the South, in a region that Mussolini believed should be part of Italy's sphere of influence.

Nonetheless, Mussolini's willingness to sign the Locarno Pact, the Kellogg–Briand Pact and the Lateran Treaties (see page 50) gave Mussolini a reputation as a wise statesman, and gained him Britain and France's respect.

## Spectrum of success

Below are a sample exam-style question and a list of general points which could be used to answer the question. Use your own knowledge and the information on the opposite page to reach a judgement about the success of the events listed. Write numbers on the spectrum below to indicate their relative success. Having done this, write a brief justification of your placement, explaining why some of these policies are more successful than others. The resulting diagram could form the basis of an essay plan.

How successful was Mussolini's foreign policy in the years 1922–29?

1. The Corfu incident
2. The Annexation of Fiume
3. The Locarno Pact
4. The Kellogg–Briand Pact

← ─────────────────────────────────────── →

Less successful                                    Very successful

## Identify an argument

Below are a series of definitions, a sample exam-style question and two sample conclusions. One of the conclusions achieves a high level because it contains an argument. The other achieves a lower level because it contains only description and assertion. Identify which is which. The mark scheme on page 3 will help you.

- Description: a detailed account.
- Assertion: a statement of fact or an opinion which is not supported by a reason.
- Reason: a statement which explains or justifies something.
- Argument: an assertion justified with a reason.

How successful was Mussolini's foreign policy in the years 1922–29?

### Sample 1

Overall, Mussolini's foreign policy in the years 1922–29 was only partially successful. The Annexation of Fiume extended Italian territory in the Balkans, and Mussolini's willingness to sign international treaties gained him the respect of Britain and France. However, Britain and France remained dominant world powers, and Mussolini failed to create a new Roman Empire. In this sense, although Mussolini's foreign policy in this period saw isolated successes, he had failed to achieve his aims.

### Sample 2

In conclusion, in the period 1922–29, Mussolini's foreign policy had some successes and some failures. The Annexation of Fiume was a success, but the Corfu Incident was a failure even though the Italian press presented it as a success. In addition, Italy had signed two Pacts, the Locarno Pact and the Kellogg–Briand Pact. These treaties brought Italy into alliance with a number of other countries. In this way, in the period 1922–29, Mussolini's foreign policy had some successes and some failures.

## The Abyssinian campaign

The Abyssinian campaign led to a significant expansion of the Italian Empire and therefore increased support for the Fascist regime.

### The causes of the campaign

The campaign's causes were largely political. First, Mussolini was determined to demonstrate the success of his regime. Italy had failed to conquer Abyssinia during the First Italo–Abyssinian War of 1895–96. Mussolini hoped to prove the superiority of Fascism by succeeding where former Italian regimes had failed. Second, he wanted to use the war to distract the Italian people from Italy's ongoing economic difficulties. Finally, he hoped that a successful war would lead to a surge in Italian nationalism.

A minor border conflict, the November 1934 **Walwal Incident**, gave Mussolini a **pretext** for war. Abyssinian Emperor **Haile Selassie I** tried to negotiate and appealed to the League of Nations to resolve the dispute. However, Mussolini sabotaged the negotiations and sent large numbers of Italian troops to the region.

### The Second Italo–Abyssinian War

The Italian invasion began in October 1935. The Abyssinian forces were poorly equipped compared to the Italian forces. Nonetheless, initially, the Italian army, led by General Emilio De Bono, suffered a series of setbacks. Indeed, the Abyssinian army's Christmas Offensive forced the Italian army to retreat. Ultimately, victory was achieved after Mussolini massively escalated the Italian forces and appointed **Pietro Badoglio** to command them. Badoglio's tactics were brutal – from the end of 1935 he even used poisoned gas against Abyssinian forces. By the end of the war in May 1936, Mussolini had committed 254 aeroplanes, 595 tanks, 30,000 trucks and 4.2 million shells to the campaign.

### International reaction

The Caribbean intellectual **C L R James** founded the International African Friends of Ethiopia. The organisation encouraged African Americans to put pressure on the US government to support the Abyssinian government.

Mussolini's reputation as a moderate leader ended with the Abyssinian campaign. It led to the deterioration of relations with Britain and France, as Italy refused to work with the two powers to find a peaceful resolution.

The League of Nations condemned the campaign and imposed economic sanctions on Italy. The sanctions failed to stop the fighting but strengthened Italy's relationship with Nazi Germany, as Germany was not part of the League and therefore continued to trade with Italy.

### Domestic reaction

The war was the high point of the Cult of the Duce (see page 40) as the press and propaganda focused on Mussolini's role directing the battle. At the end of the war, the League of Nations lifted its sanctions, leading Mussolini to claim he had beaten the entire League.

British and French attacks on the campaign were presented as hypocritical. The press argued that the British and French had no right to criticise Italian imperialism because they had large numbers of colonies and had historically fought major wars in Africa. Censorship ensured that the Italian people learned nothing of the campaign started by the International African Friends of Ethiopia.

The success of the campaign persuaded Mussolini that an aggressive foreign policy was the key to sustaining the Fascist regime. However, in the long run, Mussolini's foreign policy would take Italy into the Second World War and ultimately destroy the regime.

## Delete as applicable

Below are a sample exam-style question and a paragraph written in answer to this question. Read the paragraph and decide which of the possible options (underlined) is most appropriate. Delete the least appropriate options and complete the paragraph by justifying your selection.

How far did Fascist foreign policy increase Mussolini's popularity in the years 1922–41?

> The Abyssinian Campaign of 1935–36 increased Mussolini's popularity within Italy to a <u>great/fair/limited</u> extent. Italy's invasion of Abyssinia was successful, and Abyssinia became part of Italian East Africa. Additionally, the economic sanctions that the League of Nations imposed on Italy during the campaign were removed at the end of the campaign, allowing Mussolini to claim that the League had also been defeated. These events suggested that the Fascists would be successful in their aim of turning Italy into a great nation and therefore strengthened the popularity of the regime within Italy. Also, Mussolini's personal popularity was increased as the Italian press and propaganda focused on his role directing the war. In this way, the Abyssinian Campaign of 1935–36 increased Mussolini's popularity within Italy to a <u>great/fair/limited</u> extent because
>
> _____
>
> _____

## Support or challenge?

Below is a sample exam-style question which asks how far you agree with a specific statement. Below this are a series of general statements which are relevant to the question. Using your own knowledge and the information on the opposite page, decide whether these statements support or challenge the statement in the question and tick the appropriate box.

'The Abyssinian campaign of 1935–36 successfully increased Italy's international prestige.' How far do you agree with this statement?

| | Support | Challenge |
|---|---|---|
| Abyssinia became part of Italian East Africa. | | |
| Italy's relationship with Britain and France deteriorated. | | |
| Italy's relationship with Germany strengthened. | | |
| The League of Nations condemned the campaign and imposed economic sanctions on Italy. | | |
| The League of Nations withdrew its sanctions following the Italo–Abyssinian war. | | |
| The Italian press presented Britain and France as hypocritical for criticising Italian imperialism. | | |
| Mussolini became convinced of the need for an aggressive foreign policy. | | |

# Italian involvement in the Spanish Civil War

The Spanish Civil War of 1936 to 1939 strengthened the relationship between Mussolini and Hitler. At the same time it drove Italy further apart from Britain and France.

## Civil war in Spain

In July 1936 Spain's nationalist Army leaders launched a military coup to try to overthrow the democratically elected republican government. The League of Nations passed a resolution early on to forbid other countries from getting involved in the war. However, as the conflict progressed, Stalin's Russia intervened to support the Republicans, and both Fascist Italy and Nazi Germany sent troops and equipment to help the Nationalists.

## The causes of Italian intervention

Mussolini supported the Nationalists for a variety of reasons:

- He wanted further military success following the popularity of the victory in Abyssinia.
- He believed that the Nationalists would become Italy's allies, and help Italy gain control over the Mediterranean.
- He wanted to stop a socialist or communist victory in Spain.
- He wanted to test Italian equipment and tactics as part of his preparation for future wars.
- He believed that the Nationalists would introduce Fascism in Spain.

## The scale of Italian intervention

Mussolini sent a significant amount of military equipment to aid the Nationalists. In the first three months of the war, Italy provided:

- 130 aircraft
- 2500 tonnes of bombs
- 500 cannons
- 700 **mortars**
- 12,000 machineguns
- 4000 vehicles.

Additionally, in December 1936, Italy sent *the Corpo Truppe Volontarie* (a force of 75,000 volunteers) to fight alongside the Nationalists.

## The consequences of the war

Italian propaganda presented the Nationalist victory in 1939 as a Fascist victory over the forces of socialism and communism. However, Italy was also weakened by its involvement in the war.

At home, the campaign was not as popular as the Abyssinian campaign. The Civil War, unlike the Abyssinian campaign, lasted for three years and led to no territorial gains. Consequently, the Italian public were less enthusiastic.

The war further soured Italy's relationship with Britain and France. Consequently, Mussolini could no longer hope to negotiate territorial deals with either country in Africa or the Mediterranean.

Spain proved to be a poor ally. When Germany invaded Poland in 1939 and caused the outbreak of the Second World War, the Nationalist government refused to allow the Italian navy to use its ports. Italy's help during the Civil War did not lead to greater influence in the Mediterranean.

Italian involvement in the war also led to huge debts. The Italian government estimated that it spent 7,500,000,000 lire (approximately £8,300,000,000) on the conflict. Privately, Badoglio argued that the war was a waste of money, as Italy should have spent the money on modernising its armed forces. General Balbo (see page 50), who had been placed in charge of Italy's colonies, was also critical, arguing that the money would have been better spent consolidating Italian rule in Africa. Additionally, at the end of the war Italian forces left around a third of their equipment in Spain, further draining the resources of the Spanish army.

Finally, involvement in the war deepened Italy's relationship with Germany. As the Civil War progressed, Mussolini and Hitler collaborated on the campaign. Communication between the two governments increased and by 1939 the two countries were allies.

## Complete the Venn diagram

Use the information in this section so far to add detail to the Venn diagram below. On one side of the diagram, list the foreign policy initiatives that increased Mussolini's popularity in Italy. On the other side of the diagram, list the foreign policy initiatives that decreased Mussolini's popularity in Italy. In the centre, list the foreign policy initiatives that had a mixed effect on Mussolini's popularity.

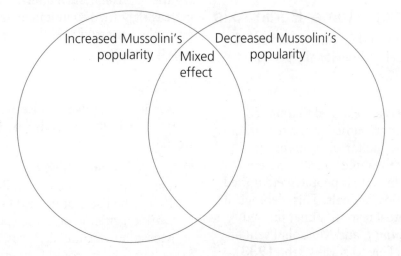

Increased Mussolini's popularity

Mixed effect

Decreased Mussolini's popularity

 ## Turning assertion into argument

Below are a sample exam-style question and a series of assertions. Read the exam question and then add a justification to each of the assertions to turn it into an argument.

How successful was Mussolini's foreign policy in the years 1922–39?

The Annexation of Fiume was a major success in the sense that

_____

_____

The Abyssinian Campaign was a partial success in the sense that

_____

_____

Italian involvement in the Spanish Civil War was only a partial success in the sense that

_____

_____

## Rome–Berlin Axis

From the mid-1930s Italy and Germany grew closer. The result was the Pact of Steel, a military alliance between Nazi Germany and Fascist Italy.

### The reasons for the Rome–Berlin Axis

The **Axis** between Italy and Germany came about for ideological, political and personal reasons.

### Ideology

Ideologically, there was a great deal that united Mussolini and Hitler. Both aimed at the rebirth of their nation, both were militarists, both hated communism, and both wanted to create a new dynamic empire in which their people were united behind common nationalist goals. This ideological similarity led to a mutual respect. Hitler praised Mussolini in *Mein Kampf*, and Mussolini sent a senior member of the PNF to speak at the **1933 Nazi Conference** in Nuremburg.

### Politics

Initially, the relationship between Nazi Germany and Fascist Italy was strained because the two counties had competing interests. Mussolini feared that a strong Germany would dominate Austria, a country that he believed should be in the Italian sphere of influence.

However, in the mid-1930s Italy and Germany became closer. Germany supported Italy's invasion of Abyssinia. Britain and France, by contrast, asked the League of Nations to impose sanctions. Furthermore, the Spanish Civil War united Italy and Germany, and further alienated Italy from Britain and France.

### Personality

Mussolini and Hitler's first meeting in 1934 was not a success. Hitler was not impressed by the achievements of Fascism and Mussolini found Hitler underwhelming. However, the two dictators collaborated effectively during the Spanish Civil War. The relationship deepened following Mussolini's trip to Germany in 1937. Mussolini was won over by Hitler's **charisma** and truly impressed by the apparent power and discipline of the Nazi regime. Consequently, after 1937 Mussolini increasingly tried to imitate Nazi Germany. For example, he introduced the German **goose step** into the Italian Army.

### Alliance

Mussolini first spoke of a Rome–Berlin Axis in November 1936. The Axis was formalised by two treaties:

- The Anti **Comintern** Pact: Germany and Japan signed the Anti Comintern Pact in November 1936. The Pact committed Germany and Japan to work together to stop the spread of communism. Mussolini was initially wary of signing the Pact as he feared it would further alienate Britain and France. However, he signed the Pact in November 1937.

- The Pact of Steel: Signed in May 1939, the Pact formed a military alliance between Italy and Germany. It committed the two countries to fight together in any future war, and to increase their collaboration in the areas of economic and military preparation for war.

### Over commitment

Mussolini's willingness to sign the Pact of Steel reflected his belief that Fascism was the force of the future. The experience of the Abyssinian campaign and the Spanish Civil War taught him that Fascist forces would always conquer democracies.

However, in reality, Italy was inadequately prepared for war. Mussolini's generals believed that Italy would not be ready for war until 1943. Moreover, Hitler's foreign policy was clearly heading in the direction of war. In this sense, signing the Pact of Steel was extremely dangerous, because Mussolini had agreed to fight alongside Germany at a time when the Italian military were unlikely to win a war.

## Spectrum of success

Below are a sample exam-style question and a list of general points which could be used to answer the question. Use your own knowledge and the information on the opposite page to reach a judgement about the success of the events listed. Write numbers on the spectrum below to indicate their relative success. Having done this, write a brief justification of your placement, explaining why some of these policies are more successful than others. The resulting diagram could form the basis of an essay plan.

How successful was Mussolini's foreign policy in the years 1922–39?

1. The Corfu incident
2. The Annexation of Fiume
3. Signing of the Locarno Pact and the Kellogg–Briand Pact
4. The Abyssinian campaign
5. Involvement in the Spanish Civil War
6. The Pact of Steel

⟵―――――――――――――――――――――――――――――⟶

Less successful                                      Very successful

## You're the examiner (a)

Below are a sample exam-style question and a paragraph written in answer to this question. Read the paragraph and the mark scheme provided on page 3. Decide which level you would award the paragraph. Write the level below, along with a justification for your choice.

How accurate is it to say that ideological factors were the main reason why Italy entered into an alliance with Germany?

> In November 1937, Mussolini signed the Anti Comintern Pact. This Pact had been signed by Germany and Japan in 1936 and committed the two countries to work together to stop the spread of communism. In addition, in 1939, Mussolini and Hitler signed the Pact of Steel. This formed a military alliance between Italy and Germany, committing them to fight together in any future war and support each other in preparation for war. Mussolini signed the Pact of Steel because he believed he liked Hitler and was impressed with Nazi Germany.

Level:          Reason for choosing this level:

_____

_____

## War and downfall

Revised

### German victories

For the first year of the Second World War Germany made enormous territorial gains, first conquering Poland, then Belgium, the Netherlands, Luxembourg and France.

The Pact of Steel (see page 64) committed Italy to fighting alongside Germany. However, the Italian military and the Italian economy were in no state to support a war. Therefore Italy could not join the war in 1939.

### Tensions in the Italian government

Powerful figures in the Italian government did not share Mussolini's faith in Hitler. At the end of 1939 the King, Foreign Minister Ciano, and Balbo believed that Italy should stay out of the war. However, Hitler's early successes persuaded most of senior figures in the government to support Mussolini's plans to join the war.

### Italy enters the war

Italy entered the war in July 1940. Mussolini rushed to enter the war, believing that the war would soon be over and that Italy should join or risk missing its chance to fight and share in the victory.

### The Italian military

The Italian army was unprepared for war. In terms of equipment, the army did not have enough uniforms to clothe its soldiers, nor was its equipment up-to-date. Additionally, Italian military tactics were outdated. Mussolini's generals had yet to develop effective strategies for using tanks and aircraft.

### Early campaigns

In 1940, Mussolini scored two **propaganda victories**:

- Italian forces played a role in the defeat of France.
- Mussolini sent 300 aircraft to take part in the **Battle of Britain**.

However, in reality the Italian military had achieved little. Italy already had **de facto** control of Albania, and therefore the Albanian campaign was largely a propaganda exercise. Although the Italian army was eventually successful in the south of France, this victory owed more to German strength than Italy's contribution. Finally, Hitler made sure that Italian aircraft only played a minor role in the air war against Britain.

### Military failures

The Italian military proved unable to achieve Mussolini's war goals:

- The Italian invasion of Greece in October 1940 was a disaster. Greece counterattacked, successfully invading Albania. Italian defeat was only avoided by the German invasion of Greece.
- British forces defeated the Italian army in East African. Again, German troops saved Italy from complete collapse until the 1943 **Battle of El Alamein** which resulted in an **Allied** victory in Africa.

### Mussolini's downfall

#### Public opinion

The Italian people had never been enthusiastic about entering the Second World War. Repeated military failures and the economic problems created by the war led to a sharp decline in Mussolini's popularity.

#### Military defeat

Having defeated Italy in North Africa, the Allies invaded Sicily in July 1943 and started bombing Rome. Nonetheless, Mussolini refused to admit defeat. Consequently, senior figures in the Italian government moved to overthrow the Duce. At the end of July the Fascist Grand Council (see page 36) met and stripped Mussolini of his military power. Following the meeting, the King sacked Mussolini and ordered his arrest, appointing Badoglio as the new Prime Minister. Badoglio's government withdrew from the Axis and joined with the Allies.

## Simple essay style

Below are two sample exam-style questions. Use your own knowledge and the information on the opposite page to produce plans for these questions. Choose four general points, and provide three pieces of specific information to support each general point. Once you have planned each essay, write the introduction and conclusion for the essay. The introduction should list the points to be discussed in the essay. The conclusion should summarise the key points and justify which point was the most important.

How far did Mussolini increase the international status of Italy in the period 1922–43?

How far do you agree that Mussolini's foreign policy strengthened his power within Italy?

## Introducing an argument

Below are a sample exam-style question, a list of key points to be made in the essay, and a simple introduction and conclusion for the essay. Read the question, the plan, and the introduction and conclusion. Rewrite the introduction and the conclusion in order to develop an argument.

To what extent was Mussolini's foreign policy in the years 1922–43 a failure?

### Key points

- The Corfu incident
- The Annexation of Fiume
- Signing of the Locarno Pact and the Kellogg–Brand Pact
- The Abyssinian Campaign
- Involvement in the Spanish Civil War
- The Pact of Steel
- Italian involvement in the Second World War

### Introduction

There were seven significant events in Italian foreign policy in the period 1922–43. These were the Corfu Incident, the Annexation of Fiume, the signing of the Locarno Pact and the Kellogg–Brand Pact, the Abyssinian Campaign, Italian involvement in the Spanish Civil War, the Pact of Steel and Italian involvement in the Second World War. Some of these events were failures, but some were successes.

### Conclusion

In some ways Italian foreign policy in the period 1922–43 was a failure and in some ways it was a success.

## Recommended reading

Below is a list of suggested further reading on this topic.

- *Italy: The Rise of Fascism 1915–1945*, chapters 8 and 9, Mark Robson (2006)
- *Mussolini and Italy*, pages 97–137 and 212–223, Edward Townley (2002)
- *Mussolini's Italy: Life Under the Dictatorship*, chapters 14 and 15, R J B Bosworth (2006)

## Exam focus

Below is a sample A grade essay. Read it and the examiner comments around it.

How far were Mussolini's foreign policy successes responsible for the popularity of the Fascist regime in the years 1922–41?

Mussolini's foreign policy successes, particularly the Abyssinian Campaign, were the main reason for the popularity of the regime in the 1930s. However, Mussolini had few foreign policy successes in the 1920s, and therefore other factors such as his accommodation with the Roman Catholic Church and his campaign against communism are more likely to explain the regime's popularity in the 1920s. Certainly, Mussolini's economic policy contributed little to the popularity of the regime as living standards either stagnated or declined for the majority of Italians in the years 1922–41.

Between 1922 and 1941 Mussolini's foreign policy had two major successes, both of which strengthened the popularity of the Fascist regime. The first was the Annexation of Fiume. In March 1923 Mussolini sent Italian troops into the Adriatic port of Fiume. He claimed that they were there to stop a revolution. However, in reality he ordered the occupation of Fiume in order to gain control of the area. The policy was a success and Italy's control of Fiume was secured by the Treaty of Rome which Italy signed with Yugoslavia in 1924. This was clearly a success for Mussolini as Italian control of Fiume was a key objective for Italian nationalists, because it was one of Mussolini's key territorial goals, and because the Italian people had shown their support for a takeover of Fiume during D'Annunzio's occupation of Fiume in 1919. This was a major foreign policy success and increased the popularity of the regime because it allowed Mussolini to claim that Fascism had achieved something that liberal politicians had failed to do in their negotiations over the Treaty of St Germain at the end of the First World War, or Giolitti's negotiation over the Treaty of Rapallo in 1920.

Another key success was the Abyssinian Campaign of 1935–36. Mussolini's objective was to extend the Italian Empire in Africa by conquering Abyssinia. The campaign started in October 1935. By May 1936, Italian forces, led by Pietro Badoglio, had defeated the forces of Haile Selassie I. Again this was a success because it achieved Mussolini's objective of extending the Italian Empire. The Italian media also claimed that it demonstrated the excellence of the Italian Army, and the use of 254 aeroplanes, 595 tanks, 30,000 trucks and 4.2 million shells showed Italy's military strength. Additionally, Mussolini refused to back down even when the League of Nations condemned the invasion. Consequently, Mussolini could claim he had beaten not only Abyssinia, but the League of Nations. Therefore, the Abyssinian Campaign, Mussolini's greatest foreign policy success, was clearly responsible for the popularity of the regime because Mussolini had shown that he could extend Italy's Empire and stand up to the League of Nations.

Other foreign policy successes did not lead to a major increase in the regime's popularity. For example, Italy's involvement in the Spanish Civil War from the middle of 1936 did not lead to increasing popularity. This is because, unlike the Abyssinian Campaign, Italian involvement in the Spanish Civil War did not lead to a quick success or extend the Italian Empire. Equally, Italian involvement in the Second World War from July 1940 did not increase the regime's popularity because the Italian people were not enthusiastic about fighting such a major war, and because by 1941, Italian territorial gains were small. In both cases, these later foreign policy successes were not responsible for the popularity of the Fascist regime because military success did not lead to obvious gains for Italy.

This paragraph shows a detailed knowledge of the annexation of Fiume. It also shows why the policy was a success and analyses why this led to support for the Fascist regime.

This paragraph uses precise detail to support its points.

This paragraph extends chronological range of the essay to 1941. Consequently, together with the earlier discussion of Fiume, it covers the whole period specified by the question.

However, Mussolini's foreign policy successes were not the only reason for the popularity of the Fascist regime in the years 1922–41. Propaganda and censorship also played a key role. For example, propaganda magnified Italy's successes in the Abyssinian Campaign. Due to Propaganda, the Abyssinian Campaign became the high point of the Cult of the Duce. Italian propaganda emphasised the hypocrisy of the imperialist nations such as Britain and France condemning Italy's imperial expansion, and turned Mussolini into an even greater hero in the eyes of the Italian people for standing up to the League of Nations. Censorship, organised by the High Commission, made no reference to the C L R James' campaign through the International African Friends of Ethiopia which was designed to put pressure on Italy to withdraw from Abyssinia. Clearly, Mussolini's foreign policy successes were responsible for the popularity of the Fascist regime in the years 1922–41, but propaganda and censorship played a key role emphasising Mussolini's achievements. Even so, the effects of Fascist propaganda were often quite limited. Indeed, it failed to create mass enthusiasm for Italy's successes in the Spanish Civil War or the early phase of the Second World War. Therefore it would be wrong to overstate the impact of Fascist propaganda.

Finally, there were clearly other reasons for the popularity of the regime. Fascist corporatism, for example, led to some benefits for workers such as holiday pay and sick pay. A variety of measures persuaded elite groups to back the regime. For example, the Concordat and family policies won the support of the Roman Catholic Church, and radical Fascists such as Aurelio Padovani were sidelined to win over the traditional agricultural elites. Additionally, Fascist propaganda ensured that Mussolini was widely regarded as a strong and decisive leader. In middle class areas propaganda stressed his anti-communism. More generally, the Italian press consistently used a variety of techniques to emphasise his strength. For example, photographers used various techniques to hide Mussolini's shortness, signs of age and to emphasise his physical strength. In this way, foreign policy successes were clearly not the only reason for Fascist popularity in the years 1922 to 1941 because the regime had policies and achievements that won over the major sections of Italian society.

In conclusion, Mussolini's foreign policy successes were clearly a big reason for the popularity of the Fascist regime in the years 1922–41. The successes of the Abyssinian campaign, highlighted by propaganda, clearly led to the high point of the Cult of the Duce and genuine enthusiasm for Fascism among the Italian people. Moreover, the early success of Fiume was genuinely popular and played a role in the initial consolidation of Fascist rule. Nonetheless, not all of the successes led to popularity. Indeed, only those successes that led to quick territorial gains really made the regime popular. Other aspects of the regime were more important, such as the economic gains made by the working class and the policies, such as the Concordat, which encouraged other important groups to support the regime.

This paragraph demonstrates high level skills as it concludes by weighing the relative importance of propaganda and genuine foreign policy successes.

This paragraph demonstrates a breadth of knowledge in very few words. It achieves this by discussing reasons why most of the major groups in Italian society supported the regime.

The conclusion makes an overall judgement that reflects the analysis presented in the rest of the essay. However, the assertion that other factors were more important than foreign policy successes is not fully supported.

28/30

This essay is very strong even though it does not get full marks. It considers a range of factors in considerable detail. Moreover, it is analytical throughout, and achieves sustained analysis by evaluating the relative importance of different foreign policy successes and their relationship to propaganda. However, it does not get full marks because its ultimate conclusion that other aspects of the regime were more important than foreign policy is not fully justified.

## What makes a good answer?

You have now considered four sample A grade essays. Use these essays to make a bullet-pointed list of the characteristics of an A grade essay. Use this list when planning and writing your own practice exam essays.

# Glossary

**1933 Nazi Conference** The first gathering of the Nazi Party since the formation of a Nazi dominated government in January 1933.

**Alberto De Stefani** Initially a liberal politician, De Stefani later became a Fascist and gained a seat on the Grand Council of Fascism. He served as Finance Ministry from 1922 to 1925.

**Allied** Referring to the USA, the Soviet Union and Britain, members of the Grand Alliance.

**Ameriqo Dumini** A Fascist and senior member of the cheka, he played a key role in the murder of Matteotti.

**Androgynous** Sexually ambiguous. Not clearly masculine or feminine according to traditional stereotypes.

**Annexation** The act of acquiring territory.

**Anti-clerical** Opposition to the Church.

**Anti-Semitic** Anti-Jewish.

**Antonio Salandra** A moderate liberal who, after the war, moved to the right and came to back Fascist policies. He was appointed a senator by Mussolini.

**Axis** Alliance.

**Balance of payments** The difference in total value between payments into and out of a country over a period.

**Battle of Britain** An air war between Britain and Axis forces from July to October 1940.

**Battle of El Alamein** A battle between Allied and German forces. The battle took place in Egypt in late 1942.

**Benito Mussolini** Fascist dictator of Italy from 1925 to 1943. He was initially a radical socialist, but became increasingly convinced that nationalism was the key to political power. Having supported Italy's participation in the First World War and considered leading a communist revolution in Italy, Mussolini joined the Fascists. He became Prime Minister in 1922 and established a dictatorship by the end of 1925.

**Budget deficit** Government debt.

**Candidate** A person who is standing for election as a member of parliament.

**Cartel** An association of businesses (e.g. manufacturers) or suppliers formed to maintain prices at a high level and to restrict competition.

**Catholic Action** Catholic groups who were trying to encourage a Catholic influence on society.

**Censorship** Control of the media through banning the publication or broadcast of material.

**Central powers** Comprised Germany, Austro-Hungary, the Ottoman Empire and Bulgaria. Developed from the Triple Alliance.

**Charisma** A type of power which comes from a person's personality.

**Cheka** Mussolini's bodyguards. They were named after the Russian secret police that was set up after the Communist Revolution.

**C L R James** A Caribbean intellectual, author and revolutionary.

**Coalitions** Governments that are made up of more than one political party.

**Collectivisation** The process of merging several small farms, which were in private ownership, together to create large farms under state ownership.

**Colonies** Part of an empire. Colonies are not self-governing, rather they are governed by the empire's mother country.

**Comintern** Also known as the Communist International. The organisation was set up in Russia to spread communism throughout the world.

**Concordat** Agreement or treaty, especially between the Vatican and a secular national government.

**De facto** According to fact, rather than according to the law.

**Decadent** A term used by Fascists and Nazis to describe people or things which had lost their strength due to self-indulgence.

**Demobilise** The process of discharging troops from military service.

**Depopulation** A process leading to a reduction in population.

**Deregulation** The process that ends or reduces government controls on private businesses.

**Dialect** A variety of a language.

**Divisive** Something that tends to cause division and conflict.

**Doctrine** A set of beliefs.

**Il Duce** Italian for leader. The term, unlike the term Prime Minister, was not a constitutional term and therefore implied that there were no constitutional limits on Mussolini's power.

**Electoral franchise** Those in the population who have the right to vote.

**Electoral system** A voting system.

**Emilio De Bono** Senior Italian military general and member of the Fascist Grand Council. He was involved in organising the March on Rome, and the murder of Matteotti. In 1929 he was appointed Minister of Colonial Affairs, and therefore had responsibility for the Italian Empire.

**Expansionism** The policy of expanding an empire by acquiring new territory.

**Extermination camps** Concentration camps that are explicitly designed to exterminate large numbers of people.

**Fascist Bloc** The coalition of political parties that fought the 1924 election, aiming to create a government headed by Mussolini.

**Fascist left** Radical Fascists who supported a social revolution which was designed to end the power of the traditional Italian elite. The Fascist left tended to advocate socialist policies, but unlike members of the socialist party, they also advocated extreme nationalism.

**Feudal laws** Medieval legal system that bound people to the land and gave them little individual freedom. It made wealthy landowners very powerful.

**Flappers** A term used to describe fashionable women in America in the 1920s. Flappers tended to wear bobbed hair, striking makeup and black and white clothes. They were associated with jazz clubs, smoking and lose morals. The fashion soon spread to Europe.

**Foreign Ministry** The part of the government that is responsible for dealing with other countries.

**Foro Mussolini** A key example of Fascist architecture, the Foro Mussolini is a sports venue built between 1928 and 1938. Foro Mussolini literally means Mussolini's forum. Its design was based on the ancient forums of imperial Rome.

**Fourteen Points** US President Woodrow Wilson's proposals for the basis of a peace agreement at the end of the First World War.

**Gabriele D'Annunzio** An Italian poet, writer and soldier, who became a national hero as an elite officer in the First World War. D'Annunzio, like many nationalists, was horrified by Italy's 'mutilated victory'. Therefore, in 1919 he led a band of rebel soldiers and took control of Fiume, establishing the Italian Regency of Carnaro. The radical and theatrical nature of D'Annunzio's government of Fiume was a key influence on Mussolini.

**Garibaldi** Giuseppe Garibaldi was a politician and soldier who was credited with being one of Italy's founding fathers.

**General strike** A situation in which all working people refuse to work. In practice, a general strike may not involve all workers, but will include large numbers of workers across most of the major sectors of industry.

**Giolitti period** The period from 1896 to 1912 in which the Italian economy grew and in which Giolitti dominated Italian politics.

**Giovanni Giolitti** A Liberal politician and five-time Prime Minister of Italy. After Mussolini he is the longest serving Prime Minister in Italian history.

**Goose step** A form of marching used by soldiers for military parades and ceremonies. The march originated in Germany.

**Great Depression** Prolonged economic crisis lasting from the Wall Street Crash in 1929 and continuing throughout the 1930s.

**Gross Domestic Product (GDP)** The total wealth produced by a country in a given period.

**Haile Selassie I** Emperor of Abyssinia from 1930 until Mussolini proclaimed the Italian King Emperor of Abyssinia in 1936. Haile Selassie I played a key role in alerting the League of Nations to Italy's use of chemical weapons in Abyssinia.

**Hitler's Germany** Germany under the Nazi dictatorship of Adolf Hitler between 1933 and 1945. Hitler's Germany was characterised by a single party dictatorship, a terroristic secret police and the abolition of civil rights.

***Homo fascistus*** The term literally translates as 'fascist man'. Fascists believed that the new heroic Fascist society required a new type of human being. This *homo fascistus* would be selflessly devoted to the nation, unlike bourgeois or working-class men who put their own pleasure and the interests of their class above the nation.

**Indirect taxation** Usually taxes on products that are paid at the point when a consumer buys goods.

**Indoctrinate** The process of persuading a person or a group of people to accept a set of beliefs without question.

**Inflation** A rise in the level of prices in an economy.

**Irrational** A person or an action that is motivated by impulses that are not rational.

**Irrigation schemes** Schemes to bring water to dry areas to aid with the growing of crops.

**Keynesian policies** Economic policies that are designed to promote economic growth by increasing government spending.

**Laissez-faire economics** Economic environment where transactions between private businesses are free from government restrictions, taxes and subsidies with only minimal regulation.

**Land hunger** When the population is too big for the amount of land available. This leads, for example, to people farming increasingly smaller plots and being unable to make enough money to survive.

**Land reclamation** The process of creating new land from rivers, lakes and the sea.

**League of Nations** An international organisation formed in 1920 to promote cooperation and peace.

**Libyan War of 1911–12** Also known as the Italo–Turkish War, it was a war to take the territory that became Libya from the Turks. It proved to be a very expensive war for Italy, costing nearly 1.3 million lire (1 billion more than predicted).

**Man of the people** A man who understands, loves and represents ordinary people.

**Martial law** Literally, military law. The term is usually used to refer to a situation in which ordinary people are placed under the control of the military.

**Mazzini** Giuseppe Mazzini was a journalist, writer and politician who played a key role in the unification of Italy.

**Mein Kampf** A book written by Adolf Hitler in 1924 and 1925. It sets out an account of his life and his key political beliefs.

**Military coup** Also known as a 'coup d'état', a military coup is a situation in which a government is overthrown by its own army.

**Militia** An army formed of ordinary citizens rather than professional soldiers.

**Ministry of the Interior** The part of government responsible for the law and order of the nation.

**Modernist** Modernism was a cultural movement that emerged in Europe in the late nineteenth century. In terms of architecture, modernist Italian architecture was characterised by urban buildings designed around long clean lines and geometric shapes. Modernism in Italy was also known as 'futurism'.

**Mortar** An explosive bomb.

**Motherland** The country at the centre of an empire.

**Mutinies** Rebellions in the armed forces.

**Napoleonic** Relating to the French Emperor and military leader Napoleon Bonaparte.

**National self-determination** The right of the people of a nation to determine their own political status.

**New industries** In the first half of the twentieth century, the term new industries referred to industries that produced relatively high-tech products, such as chemicals and electricity.

**Office of Public Security** The part of government that was responsible for policing and state security.

**Ostracising** The process of shunning a person.

**Overseas colonies** Colonies that are separated from the motherland by the sea.

**OVRA** The Fascist political police. The name 'OVRA' was essentially meaningless, it was designed to heighten the mystery around the force.

**Palazzo della Civiltà Italiana** A key example of Fascist architecture, the Palazzo della Civiltà Italiana was designed to be part of a bigger complex of buildings to showcase fascist strength to the world.

**Party list system** Relates to a system of voting where people vote for a party rather than a candidate.

**Party statute** The rules that governed the Fascist Party.

**Patronage** The power to control appointments to an office or the right to privileges.

**Pellagra** A vitamin deficiency disease, fatal within five years if not treated, that can result from a very restricted diet.

**Personal dictatorship** A dictatorship that is built on the power of one person.

**Piazza augusto imperatore** A key example of Fascist architecture, the Piazza augusto imperatore was built in the heart of Rome. Its location, near many sites associated with the Roman Empire, implied a link between the glory of ancient Rome and Fascist Italy.

**Pietro Badoglio** A military general who served in Italy's early twentieth-century colonial wars, both World Wars and the Second Italo–Abyssinian War.

**Polarisation** The process which leads to people becoming increasingly divided. Typically, people who were moderate become more extreme.

**Pope Pius XI** Pope from 6 February 1922 to 10 February 1939.

**Pretext** A reason that is given to justify an action. The reason is, however, not the real reason; in fact a pretext is given to hide the real reason for action.

**Privatised** When a business or service is transferred from public to private ownership.

**Profiteers** People or businesses that seek to make an unfair or excessive profit, often during wartime.

**Progressive taxation** Taxation that targets the rich to a greater extent than the poor.

**Propaganda victories** Military or political events that are not really victories or only partial victories, but are turned into outright victories by propaganda.

**Public spending** Government spending or expenditure.

**Public works** Building things for public use, often by government, such as roads, schools, hospitals, sewers.

**Purge** The removal of undesirable people from positions of power by more senior members of the government.

**Raffaele Guariglia** A senior Italian diplomat. Having served governments prior to the March on Rome, he continued to play an important role in Italian foreign policy under Mussolini.

**Raw materials** Materials such as oil, coal and iron. These are not finished goods, but are used to create finished goods.

**Real wages** A measure of how much personal income has changed. Real wages indicate the level of income in the context of inflation, and therefore indicate of the extent to which personal income has risen or fallen.

**Risorgimento** Literally meaning 'rebirth' or 'resurgence', this was the name for the cultural and literary revival in Italy after 1815, culminating in the unification of 1870.

**Roman salute** A symbol of Fascism, generally seen as based on an ancient Roman custom, adopted by D'Annunzio in his occupation of Fiume and then taken up by other Fascist leaders like Mussolini.

**Rule by decree** A style of rule often used by dictators or autocratic rulers that means the law can be changed by one person or a group quickly and with no challenges.

**Rule of law** Aims at preventing arbitrary actions by making sure that those in authority conform to established laws.

**Service sector** A part of the economy where people make money by serving people, for example in restaurants or shops.

**Share prices** The price of an individual share in a company.

**Sharecroppers** A tenant farmer who gives part of his crop as rent instead of only paying money for his tenancy.

**Shirkers** A slang term for people who are accused of not doing their job properly.

**Social Darwinists** In simple terms, people who believe that the strong deserve to survive at the expense of the weak. An ideological belief derived from Charles Darwin's theory of evolution. It implies that those who are strong have greater political rights than those who are weak.

**Sphere of influence** A geographical area in which one country dominates.

*Squadristi* Armed squads of Italian Fascists who wore black shirts as part of their uniform.

**Stalin's Russia** The period in Russia from 1928 to 1953 dominated by Stalin. Stalin's Russia was characterised by a highly oppressive dictatorship.

**Statesman** An internationally respected politician who plays a major role in world diplomacy.

**Syndicate** A local organisation of employers or employees.

**Technocrats** People who have power because of their expert knowledge.

**The Adriatic port of Fiume** A strategically significant port centred around the city of Fiume.

**Totalitarian state** A government that puts the needs of the individual citizen below those of the state and which implements repressive and controlling policies on all aspects of daily life.

*Trasformismo* The technique in Italian liberal politics of creating a flexible coalition from across the political spectrum, made necessary by the Italian political system.

**Treaty of London** A secret pact made between the Triple Entente powers (Great Britain, France and Russia) and Italy in 1915 that promised Italy certain lands, including Tyrol, Trieste and parts of the Balkans, in return for the alliance of Italy against their former allies in the Triple Alliance.

**Treaty of St Germain** The treaty signed on 10 September 1919 between the Allies and Austria which (amongst many other things) gave territory to Italy – although not as much as Italian nationalists had demanded.

**Undersecretariat of Arms and Munitions** This was later to become a full Ministry. It was a department of government that dealt specifically with arms, weaponry and ammunition.

**Unification** The process of uniting, in this case bringing together separate territories on the Italian peninsula to form a single unit – the Kingdom of Italy.

**Universal male suffrage** A system of voting rights where all adult males have the right to vote.

**Utopia** An ideal or perfect political community.

**Vatican** The official residence of the Pope in the Vatican City.

**Venereal disease** Disease that is spread through sexual activity.

**Vote rigging** The process of fixing the result of an election, by creating a false result. This can be achieved by a variety of illegal methods such as allowing people to vote multiple times, by deliberately miscounting votes or by deliberately losing votes.

**Voting shares** Shares in a company that allow the owner to play a role in directing the company through voting.

**Walwal Incident** A skirmish between Italian and Abyssinian solders near the border town of Walwal (also known as Welwel). Mussolini used the incident as a pretext for declaring war on Abyssinia.

# Answers

## Section 1: Italy 1896–1912

### Page 9, Develop the detail

Economic problems played some role in creating social discontent in Italy in the period 1896–1914. Although industrial workers benefited from industrial growth, agricultural workers suffered in this period. For example, some industries, **such as wool**, suffered from a lack of modern machinery. **This led to strikes, which decreased agricultural production**. In addition, many agricultural workers left to work in industry. **Between 1897 and 1912, the proportion of workers who worked in agriculture decreased from 64 per cent to 58 per cent.** Overall, incomes in rural areas of Italy barely increased. In this way, economic problems contributed to social discontent in Italy in the period 1896–1914 because they decreased standards of living for agricultural workers, and accentuated the divide between urban and rural areas.

### Page 11, Spot the mistake

The paragraph does not get into Level 4 because it does not contain detailed supporting evidence.

### Page 11, Eliminate irrelevance

One way in which regional differences in Italy did undermine the unity of the Liberal State in the period 1896–1914 was through dialect and language. People in different parts of the country spoke different forms of Italian, with the Italian spoken in the North differing considerably from the Italian spoken in the South. ~~The South was also much poorer as it was predominantly agricultural and grain prices had fallen.~~ In the 1890s, only 2 per cent of the Italian population spoke Italian, while 98 per cent spoke in local dialects. Language differences had a twofold impact on the unity of the Liberal State. First, differences in language made it difficult for Italy to develop a sense of identity. Secondly, as political power was based in the North, the language of politics was that of the North. ~~The King of Piedmont, Umberto I, had become King of Italy following unification even though he was unpopular and not very intelligent.~~ Consequently, many in the South found it hard to identify with the government. In this way, regional differences in the form of language and dialect did undermine the unity of the Liberal State in the period 1896–1914 as they prevented many people from understanding or associating themselves with the new state.

## Section 2: The impact of the First World War 1918–23

### Page 19, Complete the paragraph

Italy's 'mutilated victory' after the First World War played an important role in weakening the Liberal State in the period 1918–22. In Italy, there was widespread disappointment with the Treaty of St Germain. For example, the Italian negotiators had demanded that Italy share in the redistribution of colonies belonging to Germany and Turkey. However, this demand was refused. In addition, Italian negotiators had asked for the port of Fiume and parts of Dalmatia. This request was also refused, and these territories were given to Yugoslavia. Many in Italy believed that these terms were insulting to Italy and did not reflect Italy's role in the war. **In this way, Italy's 'mutilated victory' after the First World War played an important role in weakening the Liberal State in the period 1918–22 because it suggested that the government had not acted in the national interest, increasing dissatisfaction within Italy.**

### Page 19, Identify an argument

Sample 1 contains the argument.

### Page 21, Spot the mistake

The paragraph does not get into Level 4 because it describes the nature of the reforms and asserts that they led to dissatisfaction with the Liberal government, but it does not explain the link between the reforms and political instability. Consequently, the paragraph lacks focus on the question.

### Page 21, Develop the detail

One way in which Italy's involvement in the First World War contributed to the collapse of the Liberal State was that the war weakened confidence in Italian democracy. For example, the Prime Minister, **Antonio Salandra,** rarely allowed Parliament to meet. In addition, as a result of the war, many unelected leaders became more powerful. **Notably, military leaders gained considerable power as the government prioritised military requirements.** Consequently, the war created pressure for political reform, and radical democratic reforms were introduced **in 1919**. However, these reforms, **which introduced universal male suffrage and changed the electoral system,** created further political problems, **as political parties refused to work together to**

**gain public support**. In this way, Italy's involvement in the First World War highlighted the weaknesses of Italian democracy and led to widespread disenchantment with the Liberal State.

## Page 23, You're the examiner

The paragraph would be awarded Level 4 as it shows clear focus on the question and provides accurate, relevant and detailed supporting evidence.

## Page 23, Turning assertion into argument

The relationship between the government and big business during the war contributed to the collapse of the Liberal State because **the government failed to control businesses, creating the impression that they supported the needs of business over those of ordinary people. Consequently, they lost the support of many workers and peasants.**

The post-war economic crisis contributed to the collapse of the Liberal State because **workers and peasants blamed the government for the collapse of the economy, and turned to more radical political alternatives.**

Industrial unrest following the First World War contributed to the collapse of the Liberal State because **the middle class became afraid that the government could not control the workers, and therefore began to support anti-socialist political parties.**

## Page 27, Eliminate irrelevance

The invasion of Fiume in September 1919 played a key role in undermining the Liberal State in the years 1918–22. In this respect, the invasion was significant for three reasons. First, the invasion showed the lack of support for the government among the military. The invasion, which involved two thousand soldiers, occurred in defiance of the Liberal government, and indicated that many in the military were not loyal to the government. This had also been a problem in 1916, when many soldiers had mutinied in protest at Italian involvement in the First World War. Secondly, the invasion showed the lack of popular support for the Liberal government. Many in Italy supported the invasion, and viewed D'Annunzio as a hero. D'Annunzio was also famous for coming up with the term 'mutilated victory' to describe the view that Italy had been treated badly in the negotiations following the First World War. Thirdly, the invasion demonstrated the power of direct action, undermining the Liberal State's reliance on compromise and negotiation. In this way, the invasion of Fiume contributed to the political instability of the Liberal State in the years 1918–22 by emphasising the level of popular dissatisfaction with the Liberal government and their methods.

# Section 3: Power and control in Fascist Italy

## Page 37, Complete the paragraph

Mussolini's political appointments played a key role in the consolidation of Fascist power in Italy in the period 1922–23. For example, Mussolini appointed Fascist sympathisers to important positions. Alberto De Stefani became Finance Minister and Emilio De Bono was appointed head of the police. In addition, Mussolini appeased liberals and conservatives by giving them posts in his Cabinet. Indeed, his first Cabinet included the same number of liberals as Fascists. **In this way, Mussolini's political appointments played a key role in the consolidation of Fascist power in the period 1922–23 because they strengthened Fascist influence in government at the same time as presenting the appearance of moderation.**

## Page 41, Eliminate irrelevance

One way in which propaganda was used to consolidate Fascist power in Italy in the years 1922–29 was through the Cult of the Duce. This involved using propaganda to depict Mussolini as the saviour of Italy. For example, Mussolini was often portrayed as an all-powerful leader. He was photographed in Napoleonic poses to suggest similarities between himself and the French leader. Both Mussolini and Napoleon were said to be short. However, it is now thought that Napoleon was of average height. The government also launched a campaign with the slogan 'Mussolini is always right'. In addition, Mussolini was pictured with peasants to suggest that he was a man of the people and that he was in touch with their concerns. Furthermore, Mussolini censored the press to ensure that anti-Fascist articles were not published. In this way, the Cult of the Duce played an important role in the consolidation of Fascist power in Italy in the period 1922–29 because it persuaded many people that Mussolini's leadership was good for Italy.

## Page 41, Develop the detail

Propaganda played an important role in establishing and maintaining Fascist control over Italy in the period 1922–43. Early Fascist propaganda targeted different social groups with different messages. **For example, older voters were targeted with the message that Fascism had emerged from Italy's ancient culture.** In addition, the Cult of the Duce was used to suggest that Mussolini was a strong leader. **He was photographed excelling in sport, and was often pictured topless to show off his muscular chest.** The Cult of Rome was used to suggest that there were clear links between Fascist Italy and the Roman Empire. **For example, links were drawn between Mussolini's dictatorship and the leadership of the Roman Emperors.** Finally, modernist architecture, **such as the Esposizione Universale Roma (EUR)**, was used to suggest that the regime was creating a new Fascist utopia. In this way, propaganda was used to establish and maintain Fascist control of Italy in the period 1922–43 by encouraging people to see the regime as strong and dynamic, and drawing parallels between the Fascist regime and the Ancient Rome.

## Page 43, Turning assertion into argument

Terror played an essential role in Mussolini's consolidation of power in the sense that **it was used to intimidate voters and remove potential opponents.**

The OVRA played a key role in maintaining Fascist control of Italy in the sense that **their actions led to a widespread atmosphere of fear which discouraged opponents of Fascism.**

## Page 43, You're the examiner

The paragraph should be awarded Level 3 as it is accurate, and attempts to focus on the question, but describes the OVRA rather than explaining how it helped to establish and maintain Fascist control.

## Page 49, Develop the detail

The Battle for Grain is an example of an economic policy that was largely successful. The campaign was designed to increase grain production in Italy **with the aim of reducing grain imports and improving the balance of payments situation**. The campaign was successful at increasing grain production. **Grain production increased from an average per year of 5.5 million tonnes in the 1920s, to about 7 million tonnes in the early 1930s**. This led to a significant drop in grain imports **of 75 per cent**. However, the campaign was not entirely successful. Many farmers stopped producing citrus fruits to produce grain instead. This had an impact on the economy **as citrus fruits were an important source of income for Italy**. In this way, the Battle for Grain was very successful at meeting its aim of increasing grain production, but it had a mixed effect on Italy's balance of payments situation.

## Section 4: Building the new Roman Empire

## Page 59, Identify an argument

Sample 1 contains the argument.

## Page 63, Turning assertion into argument

The Annexation of Fiume was a major success in the sense that **it extended Italian territory in the Balkans and increased Mussolini's popularity in Italy.**

The Abyssinian Campaign was a partial success in the sense that **it extended Italian territory in East Africa achieving one of Mussolini's key foreign policy aims, but also strengthened Italy's relationship with Germany leading, ultimately, to defeat in the Second World War.**

Italian involvement in the Spanish Civil War was only a partial success in the sense that **although the Nationalists won the war, Italian involvement was expensive, unpopular in Italy, and soured Mussolini's relationship with Britain and France.**

## Page 65, You're the examiner

The paragraph should be awarded Level 2 as it contains some accurate material that is relevant to the question, but focus on the question is very weak.

# Timeline

**1896** Italian army defeated at Adowa

**1903** Giolitti becomes Prime Minister

**1910** Nationalist Congress held

**1911** Beginning of the Libyan War

**1912** Franchise extended to all literate men over 21 and all men over 30

**1914** Resignation of Giolitti

**1915** Treaty of London: Italy joins the Triple Entente

Creation of the Undersecretariat of Arms and Munitions

**1916** Mutinies in the army

**1919** Widespread industrial unrest

Creation of the Catholic Popular Party

*Fasci di Combattimento* launched

Treaty of St Germain

Democratic reforms

Invasion of Fiume by Italian nationalists

**1920** Lira worth only 20 per cent of its value in 1914

Trade union membership reaches 2 million

Treaty of Rapallo

**1921** Italian Communist Party founded

Fascists join Giolitti's 'National Block'

National Fascist Party founded

Collapse of two major munitions companies

**1922** March on Rome

Mussolini becomes Prime Minister

Mussolini granted emergency powers

Grand Council of Fascism created

**1923** Acerbo Law passed

Corfu Incident

**1924** Annexation of Fiume

General election: Fascists gain two-thirds of the seats in new Parliament

Matteotti Crisis

Film censorship introduced

**1925** Purge of teachers and lecturers who did not support Fascism

All newspaper editors forced to join Association of Fascist Journalists

Battle for Grain introduced

Locarno Pact

Mussolini given the title Duce

**1926** *Opera Nazionale Balilla* (ONB) established

Battle for the Lira introduced

Special Tribunal for the Defence of the State established

All political parties except the Fascist Party banned

OVRA established

All opposition newspapers closed

Ministry of Corporations established

Abortion and contraception outlawed

**1927** Battle for Births policy introduced

Establishment of new newspapers banned

Minculpop established

**1928** Kellogg–Briand Pact

**1929** Teachers and lecturers forced to swear an oath of allegiance to Fascism

Lateran Treaties

**1930** National Council of Corporations established

**1931** Homosexuality banned

**1932** Military salute becomes the official greeting in the civil service

**1933** Institute for Industrial Reconstruction established

**1934** Twenty-two national corporations established

**1935** Construction begins on the Esposizione Universale Roma (EUR)

Policy of autarky adopted

**1936** Birth rate begins to increase

Start of the Spanish Civil War

Italian invasion of Abyssinia

**1937** Italy signs the Anti Comintern Pact

**1938** Introduction of a 10 per cent cap on women workers in most industries

First of Mussolini's anti-Semitic laws passed

**1939** Membership of the ONB becomes compulsory

Pact of Steel

**1940** Italy enters the Second World War

**1941** Attempt to expel non-Italian Jews from Italy

**1942** Mussolini agrees to send all Jews in Italy to Nazi concentration camps

**1943** Mussolini sacked as Prime Minister and arrested